my revision notes

Edexcel A-level History

GERMANY, 1871–1990
UNITED, DIVIDED AND REUNITED

Alan Farmer

Series editor
Peter Callaghan

HODDER
EDUCATION
AN HACHETTE UK COMPANY

Acknowledgements

The Publishers would like to thank the following for permission to reproduce copyright material. **Page 48:** From *Nazism 1919–1945 Volume 1: The Rise to Power 1919–1934* (A Documentary Reader), Liverpool University Press 9780859895989.

Every effort has been made to trace all copyright holders, but if any have been inadvertently overlooked, the Publishers will be pleased to make the necessary arrangements at the first opportunity.

Although every effort has been made to ensure that website addresses are correct at time of going to press, Hodder Education cannot be held responsible for the content of any website mentioned in this book. It is sometimes possible to find a relocated web page by typing in the address of the home page for a website in the URL window of your browser.

Hachette UK's policy is to use papers that are natural, renewable and recyclable products and made from wood grown in sustainable forests. The logging and manufacturing processes are expected to conform to the environmental regulations of the country of origin.

Orders: please contact Bookpoint Ltd, 130 Milton Park, Abingdon, Oxon OX14 4SE. Telephone: +44 (0)1235 827720. Fax: +44 (0)1235 400454. Email education@bookpoint. co.uk Lines are open from 9 a.m. to 5 p.m., Monday to Saturday, with a 24-hour message answering service. You can also order through our website: www.hoddereducation.co.uk

ISBN: 9781 4718 7664 6

© Alan Farmer 2017

First published in 2017 by

Hodder Education,
An Hachette UK Company
Carmelite House
50 Victoria Embankment
London EC4Y 0DZ

www.hoddereducation.co.uk

Impression number   10 9 8 7 6 5 4 3 2 1

Year   2021 2020 2019 2018 2017

Cover photo © EyeEm Mobile GmbH/Alamy Stock Photo
Illustrations by Integra
Typeset by Integra Software Services Pvt. Ltd., Pondicherry, India
Printed in India

A catalogue record for this title is available from the British Library.

My revision planner

Key Topic 5 Reunification: recreating a united Germany, 1989–90

Part 2 Aspects in breadth: prosperity and social change, 1871–1990

Theme 1 Social change in Germany and West Germany, 1871–1990

Theme 2 Economic change in Germany and West Germany, 1871–1990

Introduction

About Paper 3

Paper 3 Germany, 1871–1990: united, divided and reunited combines a depth study of different approaches to the problem of difference with a broader thematic study of prosperity and social change. Paper 3 tests you against two Assessment Objectives: AO1 and AO2:

AO1 tests your ability to:
- organise and communicate your own knowledge
- analyse and evaluate key features of the past
- make supported judgements
- deal with concepts of cause, consequence, change, continuity, similarity, difference and significance.

On Paper 1, AO1 tasks require you to write essays from your own knowledge.

AO2 tests your ability to:
- analyse and evaluate source material from the past
- explore the value of source material by considering its historical context.

On Paper 2, the AO2 task requires you to write an essay which analyses two sources which come from the period you have studied.

Paper 3 is worth 30 per cent of your A-level.

Structure

Paper 3 is structured around two themes and five key topics.

The exam is divided into three sections, which relate to different aspects of your course:

Aspect of the course	Exam
Topic 1: Ruling the Second Reich, 1871–79	Section A (AO2) and Section B (AO1)
Topic 2: The birth of democratic Germany, 1917–19	
Topic 3: A new Reich, 1933–35	
Topic 4: Establishing and ruling the new Federal Republic, 1949–60	
Topic 5: Reunification: recreating a united Germany, 1989–90	
Theme 1: Social change in Germany and West Germany, 1871–1990	Section C (AO1)
Theme 2: Economic change in Germany and West Germany, 1871–1990	

The exam

The Paper 3 exam lasts for 2 hours and 15 minutes, and is divided into three sections.

Section A and Section B test the depth of your historical knowledge of the five topics:
- Section A requires you to answer one compulsory question concerning a single source. You should spend 15 to 20 minutes reading the source and planning your answer, and around 35 to 40 minutes writing the essay.
- Section B requires you to write one essay from a choice of two. As this is a depth paper, questions can be set on single events. Section B essays usually tests you knowledge of a shorter period than Section C. You should spend 35 to 40 minutes on Section B.

Section C requires you to answer one question from a choice of two. Questions in Section C will focus on the two themes and will cover at least 100 years. Questions can focus on either theme, or may test knowledge of both themes. You should spend 35 to 40 minutes on Section C.

How to use this book

This book has been designed to help you to develop the knowledge and skills necessary to succeed in this exam. Each section is made up of a series of topics organised into double-page spreads. On the left-hand page, you will find a summary of the key content you need to learn. Words in bold in the key content are defined in the glossary. On the right-hand page, you will find exam-focused activities. Together, these two strands of the book will take you through the knowledge and skills essential for exam success.

There are three levels of exam-focused activities.
- Band 1 activities are designed to develop the foundational skills needed to pass the exam.
- Band 2 activities are designed to build on the skills developed in Band 1 activities and to help you achieve a C grade.
- Band 3 activities are designed to enable you to access the highest grades.

Each section ends with an exam-style question and model high-level answer with commentary. This should give you guidance on what is required to achieve the top grades.

1 Ruling the Second Reich, 1871–79

The *Kaiserreich*

The Second German Empire (*Kaiserreich*) was proclaimed in January 1871 following Prussian–German success in the Franco-Prussian War. King William I of Prussia became the new German Emperor (Kaiser) with **Otto von Bismarck** as his Imperial Chancellor.

The Franco-Prussian War, 1870–71

In 1870 France and Prussia went to war. Prussia, allied with the southern German states, defeated France. The war was essentially a Prussian enterprise. Nevertheless, it was also a genuinely German war in which all the German states fought.

The German constitution

The *Kaiserreich*'s constitution incorporated the main provisions of the North German Confederation's constitution. Germany was to be a **federal state**. Powers and functions were divided between the central government and 25 state governments. The exact nature of Germany's political system after 1871 continues to be debated. Historians have variously described it as a military monarchy, a semi-**autocracy** or a constitutional monarchy.

The North German Confederation

This had been created in 1867, following Prussia's success against Austria in the Seven Weeks' War (1866). All the German states, except the southern states of Bavaria, Württemberg, Baden and Hesse-Darmstadt, joined the Confederation.

The Kaiser

The Kaiser had the power to appoint and dismiss the Chancellor and to dissolve the *Reichstag*. He controlled foreign policy, could make treaties and alliances, commanded the army and could declare war and make peace. He also supervised the execution of all federal laws.

The Chancellor

The Chancellor, the chief minister, was responsible to the Emperor, not the *Reichstag*. He chaired sessions of the *Bundesrat* and could appoint and dismiss state secretaries responsible for the various ministries.

The *Reichstag*

The *Reichstag*, the national parliament, was elected by all males over 25 years of age. It could accept or reject legislation but had only limited powers to initiate new laws. State secretaries could not sit in the *Reichstag* and were not responsible to it. *Reichstag* members were elected every five years unless the *Reichstag* was dissolved by the Kaiser.

The *Bundesrat*

The *Bundesrat* or Federal Council, comprising 58 members, was nominated by the state assemblies. Prussia had 17 members, Bavaria six and the smaller states one each. The *Bundesrat*'s consent was required in the passing of new laws. It had the power to change the constitution. However, a vote of fourteen members constituted a **veto**.

The federal government and the *Länder*

The federal or national government had responsibilities for the Reich as a whole, including matters such as defence, foreign affairs, customs, railways and the postal service.

While no longer sovereign or free to **secede**, the Reich's 25 states (or *Länder*) preserved their own constitutions and administrative systems. State governments retained considerable powers over taxation, education, police, local justice and transport. The kings of Bavaria, Saxony and Württemberg even retained their own armies.

Kaiser William I

In many respects, the key man in the 1871 constitution was the Kaiser. William I, however, was generally content to leave the task of governing Germany (and Prussia) to Bismarck and limited himself to embodying the dignity of the new state.

Conclusion

The complex system can be seen (positively) as creating a delicate equilibrium with the key institutions keeping each other in check. It can also be seen (negatively) as creating major tensions, not least between monarchical and parliamentary claims to power.

Complete the paragraph   a

Below are a sample exam-style question and a paragraph written in answer to this question. The paragraph contains a point and a concluding explanatory link back to the question, but lacks examples. Complete the paragraph, adding examples in the space provided.

How accurate is it to say that the constitution of the Second Reich in the years 1871–79 was mainly undemocratic?

> The role of the Emperor within the constitution of the Second Reich suggests that the constitution was fundamentally undemocratic. For example,
>
> _____
>
> _____
>
> Accordingly, the Emperor's role suggests that the Second Reich's constitution was fundamentally undemocratic because ultimately the Emperor had considerable power and was unaccountable to the German people.

 Eliminate irrelevance a

Below are a sample exam-style question and a paragraph written in answer to this question. Read the paragraph and identify parts of the paragraph that are not directly relevant to the question. Draw a line through the information that is not irrelevant and justify your deletions in the margin.

How accurate is it to say that the constitution of the Second Reich in the years 1871–79 was mainly democratic?

> The Reichstag, or Parliament, was clearly the most democratic element of the Second Reich's constitution. The constitution was devised by Bismarck following Prussia's — or perhaps Germany's — victory over France in 1870–71. It very much mirrored the North German Confederation, also drawn up by Bismarck, following Prussia's victory over Austria in 1866. The 1867 constitution had to be redrawn because four more states had now joined what had become the Second Reich. Bismarck, a Prussian landowner, did not have much sympathy with democracy. Nevertheless, he realised that it would be foolish to deny the German people a say in the way Germany was governed. The Reichstag ensured the people had a voice. It was elected by all men over the age of 25 and was thus far more representative than most parliaments, including Britain's, at this time. It had the power to reject, accept and amend any law. It should be said that there were limits to the power of the Reichstag. It could not introduce new laws. Nor could it elect — or eject — the Chancellor. Nevertheless, the Reichstag is evidence that there was a strong democratic element within the Second Reich's constitution.

Trying to reconcile unity and division

The *Kaiserreich* was born in a mood of national euphoria. Germans were proud of their victory over France, proof of their new country's military and economic strength. Nevertheless, the new Reich was far from united.

Disunity

- Each state had its own traditions. Each also had powers over education, justice, agriculture, religious matters and local government.
- Over 60 per cent of the population were Protestant, but Catholicism was strong especially in south-west Germany and in the Rhineland.
- Ten per cent of the Reich's population were Poles, Danes or French.
- There were economic and social divisions – between rich and poor, and between the industrialising north and west and the predominantly rural south and east.

Prussian dominance?

Bismarck intended that Prussia should dominate the new Reich. To a large extent, he succeeded in his aim:

- Prussia possessed 60 per cent of Germany's population and two-thirds of its territory. Prussia returned 235 deputies out of a total of 397 in the *Reichstag*. The fact that it had 17 seats in the *Bundesrat* meant it could block any unwelcome constitutional amendments.
- As German Emperor, the Prussian king was head of the imperial executive and civil service and supreme warlord of the Reich's armed forces.
- Imperial Chancellors were almost always simultaneously Prime Minister of Prussia.
- Prussian and imperial institutions were so intertwined that they could hardly be distinguished. The Prussian minister of war was also the imperial minister of war. Imperial secretaries of state worked closely with Prussian ministers.
- Prussia's aristocracy enjoyed a dominant position in the political, military and administrative structure of the Empire.
- The Prussian state parliament, elected by a three-class system, was dominated by the aristocracy, the rich, the military and a conservative civil service. This hindered the development of parliamentary democracy in Germany as a whole.

The Prussian state government

Prussian voters were divided into three classes, according to the amount of taxes they paid. This ensured that the rich had far more electoral power than the poor and power remained in conservative hands. Most of the other state assemblies were elected by universal suffrage.

The Germanisation of Prussia

For all the complaints about a 'Prussianisation' of Germany, the identity of 'old Prussia' was significantly diluted by its integration into the Reich. Prussia could no longer be governed without consideration of the wider interests of Germany. Prussian influence was slowly undermined by the need to make concessions to the states. Non-Prussians soon held important posts in government both in the Reich as a whole and in Prussia. It was the new Reich, not Prussia, which now engaged the loyalties of most Germans.

German nationalism

A major problem after 1871 was to unite Germany in fact as well as in theory. Pre-1871 nationalism had usually been seen as a progressive force which aimed to introduce liberal and representative government. After 1871 German nationalism became more conservative. The German nation was now identified with the new Reich, any criticism of which was denounced as unpatriotic. A distinct national identity developed that transcended that of the member states.

! Spot the mistake　　a

Below are a sample exam-style question and an introductory paragraph written in answer to this question. Why does the paragraph not get into Level 5? Once you have identified the mistake, rewrite the paragraph so that it displays the qualities of Level 5. The mark scheme on page 111 will help you.

To what extent was Germany united in the years 1871–79?

> To a large extent Germany was united after 1871. Most Germans were proud of their success in the war against France. Most Germans were Prussian and Prussia dominated the Kaiserreich. German nationalism was soon a major force in Europe.

⭥ Develop the detail　　a

Below are a sample exam-style question and a paragraph written in answer to this question from the activity above. The paragraph contains a limited amount of detail. Annotate the paragraph to add additional detail to the answer.

To what extent did Prussia control Germany in the years 1871–79?

> To a large extent Prussia did control Germany in the 1870s. William, the Prussian King, became German Emperor. Bismarck, the Prussian Prime Minister, became German Chancellor. Prussia, the biggest state, dominated both the Reichstag and the Bundesrat. Prussian aristocrats had considerable power over the German government, German administration and the German army.

The importance of the *Reichstag* and the parties

REVISED

Arguably Germany's political system was essentially autocratic, with power residing ultimately with the Emperor. But in some respects the system, by nineteenth-century standards, was remarkably democratic.

The *Reichstag*

Reichstag weaknesses

Bismarck wanted political power in Germany to remain in traditional hands: this meant in those of the Emperor and his army officers and ministers – and particularly in Bismarck's own. Arguably the constitution gave little opportunity for the exercise of democracy. The *Reichstag*, for example, could censure the Chancellor but not secure his dismissal. It could itself be dismissed at any time and new elections called. Bismarck was ready to work with the *Reichstag* only on condition that it accepted his proposals or some compromise acceptable to him. If agreement could not be reached, he could dissolve the *Reichstag* and call for fresh elections in which he used all the means at his disposal (especially the exploitation of international crises) to win backing for his measures.

Reichstag strengths

- The *Kaiserreich* needed a vast number of new laws. No bill could become a law until it passed the *Reichstag*. The government also needed more money, which only the *Reichstag* could provide. Bismarck, therefore, was forced to negotiate deals and grant concessions.

- The *Reichstag* was an open forum of debate whose members enjoyed parliamentary immunity. Debates were widely reported in the press. The Chancellor and the ministers of state could be questioned and embarrassed.
- No parliament in the world in the 1870s was elected on a broader franchise.
- What is striking is how troublesome the *Reichstag* was for Bismarck, criticising and often thwarting his plans.

Germany's main political parties

While Germany's political parties were in no position to form governments, Bismarck could not ignore them. Although under no obligation to adopt policies approved by the *Reichstag*, he did need to secure support for his own legislative proposals.

Political power

Reichstag politicians have often been criticised for failing to do more to exploit their potential power. However, the balance of power was tilted sharply in favour of the monarchy and most Germans remained deeply respectful of authority, believing that it was right and proper that the Emperor, or his Chancellor, should rule. There was no widespread conviction that power should reside with a political party which happened to have a majority of seats in the *Reichstag*.

German parties 1871–9

The National Liberals	The National Liberals, the strongest political party, drew their support from the Protestant middle class. While supporting parliamentary democracy, they also supported the creation of a strong nation-state. Until 1878 the National Liberals were Bismarck's most reliable allies.
The Centre Party	This party, which defended the interests of Catholics, became the second-largest party in the *Reichstag* in 1871.
The Social Democratic Party	In 1875 moderate and revolutionary socialists united to form the Social Democratic Party (or SPD). Its declared aim was the overthrow of the existing order. It campaigned for the nationalisation of banks, coal mines and industry and for social equality.
The German Conservative Party	This party, mainly composed of Prussian landowners, was initially sceptical about German unification.
The Free Conservatives	Drawn from a wider geographical and social base than the German Conservatives, the Free Conservatives contained not just landowners but also industrialists.
The Progressives	This was a liberal party. But unlike the National Liberals, it was opposed to Bismarck's authoritarian methods.

! Simple essay style

Below is a sample exam-style question. Use your own knowledge and the information on the opposite page to produce a plan for this question. Choose four general points, and provide three pieces of specific information to support each general point. Once you have planned your essay, write the introduction and conclusion for it. The introduction should list the points to be discussed in the essay. The conclusion should summarise the key points and justify which point was the most important.

To what extent was the Second Reich a democratic state in the years 1871–79?

i Introducing an argument

Below are a sample exam-style question, a list of key points to be made in the essay and a simple introduction and conclusion for the essay. Read the question, the plan and the introduction. Rewrite the introduction and conclusion in order to develop an argument.

To what extent did political parties have real power in Germany in the years 1871–79?

Key points

- The 1871 constitution
- *Reichstag* weaknesses
- *Reichstag* powers
- The political parties
- Bismarck's need for political support

Introduction

The Second Reich is often seen as an entrenched autocracy with real power in the hands of the Emperor and his Chancellor. However, the Second Reich's constitution established a German parliament, or *Reichstag*. This body, elected by all men over 25, was able to accept, reject or amend legislation. These were real powers.

Conclusion

Thus, there is clear evidence that political parties in Germany in the 1870s had real power. Bismarck may have had more power but he needed political party support if he was to pass measures through the *Reichstag*.

The impact of regional and social divisions

REVISED

Regional divisions

Bismarck and his **allies**, the National Liberals, were anxious to create a united Germany. Several regional obstacles stood in the way.

The problem of southern Germany

Many southern Germans disliked Prussia and (what they saw as) Prussian rule. The fact that most southern Germans were Catholics while most northern Germans were Protestants did not help matters. Nor did Bismarck's clash with the Catholic Church – the *Kulturkampf* (see page 16).

The problem of the national minorities

There were three large national minorities in Germany: Poles (in the east), Danes (in Schleswig-Holstein) and French (in Alsace-Lorraine). Bismarck regarded these groups as potential 'enemies of the state'. He thus sought to reduce their influence:

- The Polish language was outlawed in education and law courts.
- Alsace-Lorraine became a special region under direct imperial rule with a governor and Prussian civil servants. The German language was imposed in schools and local administration.

However, Bismarck did not rely solely on repression. Those French who disliked German rule, for example, were allowed to leave. The national minorities' alienation from the Reich probably lessened over the years. School, conscription and everyday experience 'Germanised' many minorities.

Social division

Growing industrial development after 1871 swelled the ranks of Germany's industrial working class. This had political as well as economic consequences. Many of the **proletariat** were attracted to socialism.

Bismarck and socialism

Bismarck regarded socialists as dangerous revolutionaries and a threat to the kind of society he intended to maintain. In 1876 he tried to pass a bill preventing the publication of socialist propaganda. It was defeated.

In May 1878 an anarchist tried to assassinate Emperor William I. The would-be assassin had no proven association with the SPD, but Bismarck, like many of his contemporaries, drew no distinction between anarchism and socialism and saw the murder attempt as part of a 'red' conspiracy. However, his efforts to push through a bill against socialism were defeated by National Liberals who were concerned about civil liberties.

A second attempt on William's life a week later resulted in the Emperor being seriously wounded. Again the failed assassin had no direct SPD link. But Bismarck criticised the National Liberals for failing to pass the anti-socialist bill that might have protected the Emperor. Scenting political advantage, he dissolved the *Reichstag*. The electorate, deeply shocked by the murder attempts, blamed the SPD and the National Liberals. The SPD vote fell from 493,000 in 1877 to 312,000 while the National Liberals lost 130,000 votes.

Bismarck's actions against socialism

An anti-socialist bill, supported by Conservatives and most National Liberals, was passed by the new *Reichstag* in 1878:

- Socialist organisations, including trade unions, were banned.
- Socialist meetings were forbidden.
- Socialist publications were outlawed.

The anti-socialist law, far from eliminating socialism, served to rally the faithful and fortify them in their beliefs. Moreover, the law, differently implemented in different German states, did not prevent SPD members from standing for election and speaking freely in both the *Reichstag* and state legislatures. In the 1880s Bismarck tried to wean the working classes from socialism by introducing various welfare (state socialism) measures, such as old age pensions, designed to assist German workers. While his measures became a model of social provision for other countries, many German workers believed them a sham and SPD support continued to increase.

Mind map

Use the information on the opposite page to add detail to the mind map below so that you gain a greater understanding of the divisions in Germany after 1871.

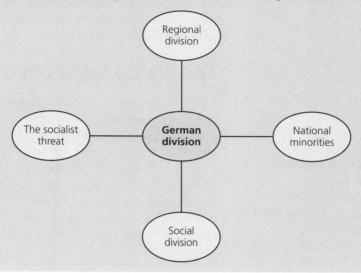

 Spectrum of significance

Below are a sample exam-style question and a list of general points which could be used to answer the question. Use your own knowledge and the information on the opposite page to reach a judgement about the importance of these general points to the question posed. Write numbers on the spectrum below to indicate their relative importance. Having done this, write a brief justification of your placement, explaining why some of these factors are more important than others. The resulting diagram could form the basis of an essay plan.

To what extent were socialists the greatest threat to German unity in the years 1871–79?

1 Regional divisions

2 The problem of national minorities

3 Social divisions

4 The rise of socialism

5 Bismarck's actions against socialists

Socialism – the greatest threat   Other threats more important

Bismarck as Imperial Chancellor, 1871–79

Bismarck's power

After 1871 Bismarck was Prussian Prime Minister and Foreign Minister and Imperial Chancellor. His reputation as the man who had brought about German unification coupled with his influence over William I gave him an immensely strong position. Bismarck, who loathed the existence of any rival authority, ensured that other ministers were little more than senior clerks, carrying out his orders.

Realpolitik

Realpolitik characterised Bismarck's political career. What was good for Prussia/Germany was good. In his view, the end justified the means and he had little time for idealism or idealists. Recognising that a conservative regime could no longer operate without popular support, he hoped to achieve conservative ends by means that were often far from conservative. His methods occasionally brought him into conflict with William I and the Prussian élites. But while many distrusted his tactics, most respected his judgement.

Limitations to Bismarck's power

Bismarck was not always successful in his efforts to shape domestic developments.
- The fact that Germany was a federal state reduced his influence.
- The *Reichstag* was a major constraint.

Bismarck's long absences from Berlin (he liked to spend time on his country estates) and his poor health (often stomach troubles arising from over-eating and over-drinking) reduced his control of day-to-day decision-making.

Bismarck's co-operation and eventual break with the National Liberals

Bismarck claimed to stand above party or sectional interest. Nevertheless, he needed a parliamentary majority. Although he was by no means a liberal, he worked with the National Liberals, the *Reichstag*'s strongest party, for most of the 1870s. In some respects the National Liberals were ideal allies. Most were eager to help him consolidate national unity. A great deal of useful legislation was passed:
- A national currency was introduced.
- A **Reichsbank** was created.
- All internal tariffs were abolished.
- There was much legal standardisation.

Nevertheless, relations between Bismarck and the National Liberals were uneasy. Bismarck did not agree with their hopes for the extension of parliamentary government and also was irritated by their opposition to some of his proposals, including the army budget.

The War in Sight crisis

Bismarck was prepared to use nationalism to rally support. In 1875, for example, he provoked a diplomatic crisis by claiming that France was planning a war of revenge against Germany. His move won him popular support in Germany. However, it was not a great diplomatic success. Britain and Russia warned Germany about its provocative actions, forcing Bismarck to offer assurances that Germany was not contemplating war with France.

Economic protectionism

In the early 1870s Bismarck supported **free trade**, an essential principle of the National Liberals. In 1879, however, he ditched both free trade and the National Liberals.

Economic and financial factors

- There were strong economic reasons for introducing protective tariffs (see page 96).
- The federal government's revenue, raised from customs duties and indirect taxation, did not cover the growing costs of armaments and administration. In order to make up the deficit, supplementary payments were made by individual states. Bismarck hoped that new tariffs would ensure that the federal government was financially independent of the states and the *Reichstag*.

Political factors

By the late 1870s many Germans were clamouring for protective tariffs. By espousing protectionist policies, Bismarck realised he could broaden his political support. In the 1878 elections, the National Liberals lost some 30 seats. Protectionists, made up mostly of Conservatives and Centre Party members, had a majority in the *Reichstag*.

The 1879 Tariff Act

In 1879 a tariff bill passed through the *Reichstag*, imposing duties on imports. The political results were far-reaching.
- Bismarck was now firmly committed to the Conservative camp.
- The National Liberals splintered. Some united with the Progressives. Others remained loyal to Bismarck.

Simple essay style

Below is a sample exam-style question. Use your own knowledge and the information on the opposite page to produce a plan for this question. Choose four general points, and provide three pieces of specific information to support each general point. Once you have planned your essay, write the introduction and conclusion for the essay. The introduction should list the points to be discussed in the essay. The conclusion should summarise the key points and justify which point was the most important.

> How accurate is it to say that Bismarck and the National Liberals were natural allies in the years 1871–79?

 Support or challenge?

Below is a sample exam-style question which asks how far you agree with a specific statement. Below this is a series of general statements which are relevant to the question. Using your own knowledge and the information on the opposite page, decide whether these statements support or challenge the statement in the question and tick the appropriate box.

> 'Bismarck and the National Liberals were natural allies.' How far do you agree with this statement about Bismarck's relationship with the National Liberals in the years 1871–79?

	SUPPORT	CHALLENGE
Bismarck preferred to rule as an autocrat.		
The National Liberals were the strongest party in the *Reichstag* from 1871–78.		
Bismarck needed *Reichstag* support.		
Most National Liberals believed in national unity.		
Most National Liberals believed in parliamentary democracy.		
The National Liberals lost support in the 1878 elections.		
Bismarck supported protective tariffs in 1879.		
Many National Liberals continued to support Bismarck after 1879.		

The *Kulturkampf*

The 1870s were dominated by Bismarck's clash with the Catholic Church – the *Kulturkampf*.

Reasons for the *Kulturkampf*

In the late nineteenth century the Catholic Church seemed to be a reactionary force.

- In 1864 the papacy condemned every major principle for which liberals stood, such as democracy and religious liberty.
- In 1870 the Vatican Council laid down the doctrine of **papal infallibility**.

German Protestants and liberals were alarmed. They feared that militant Catholicism would interfere in the Reich's affairs.

Bismarck's motives

Bismarck, a sincere Protestant, viewed Catholics with suspicion. Determined to unify the new Reich, he was aware that many of those who opposed unification, especially southern Germans who still identified with Austria, were Catholic. Bismarck saw the (Catholic) Centre Party's success in 1871 as a danger to the Empire's unity. He feared that Centre politicians would encourage civil disobedience among Catholics whenever state policies conflicted with those of the Church.

The *Kulturkampf* was regarded at the time as a war against internal opponents of unification. It may also have been a calculated political ploy on Bismarck's part. The fact that he put himself at the head of a popular Protestant crusade enabled him to work closely with the National Liberals in the 1870s.

The 'Old Catholics'

Some 5,000 'Old Catholics', refusing to accept the decree on papal infallibility, broke with the Church. When Old Catholic teachers and professors were dismissed by Catholic bishops, Bismarck had an excellent excuse to attack the Church in 1872.

Actions against the Church

While the *Kulturkampf* was centred on Prussia, its effects were felt throughout the Reich. Anti-Catholic legislation was passed in Prussia, by other state governments and by the *Reichstag*.

In 1872:
- Catholic schools were brought under state supervision
- The *Reichstag* banned **Jesuits** from Germany.

In 1873 Adalbert Falk, Prussian Minister of Religion and Education, introduced a package of measures, known as the May Laws:
- All priesthood candidates had to attend a **secular university** before commencing training.
- All religious appointments became subject to state approval.
- In 1874 obligatory civil marriage was introduced in Prussia.
- In 1875 all religious orders, except nursing orders, were dissolved.

Clergy could be fined, imprisoned and expelled if they failed to comply with the legislation. By 1876 all but two of the 12 Prussian Catholic bishops were in exile or under house arrest. More than 1,000 priests were suspended.

Failure of the *Kulturkampf*

- Attempts to repress Catholicism met with considerable opposition. Catholic communities fiercely maintained their religious culture.
- Bismarck's hope of destroying the Centre Party backfired: the *Kulturkampf* strengthened rather than weakened his opponents. In 1871 the Centre won 58 seats; in 1874 it won 91.

The end of the *Kulturkampf*

By 1878 Bismarck accepted that the *Kulturkampf* had failed. It had increased disunity between the Reich and its Catholic subjects, not removed it. Pope Pius IX's death in 1878 gave Bismarck an opportunity to backtrack. Negotiations with Pope Leo XIII led to improved relations between Bismarck and the Church. Falk was dismissed in 1879 and some – but by no means all – anti-Catholic measures were repealed. Typically, Bismarck sought to turn a setback to his advantage by winning Centre Party support for his conservative, protectionist and anti-socialist measures.

Mind map

Use the information on the opposite page to add detail to the mind map below. This should provide you with a greater understanding of the causes, course and consequences of the *Kulturkampf*.

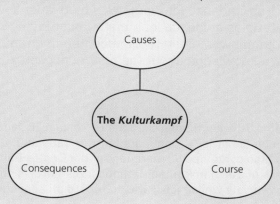

RAG – rate the timeline

Below are a sample exam-style question and a timeline. Read the question, study the timeline and, using three coloured pens, put a Red, Amber or Green star next to the events to show:

Red: events and policies that have no relevance to the question

Amber: events and policies that have some significance to the question

Green: events and policies that are directly relevant to the question

1 To what extent was the *Kulturkampf* a politically inspired move by Bismarck in the years 1871–79?

Now repeat the activity with the following question:

2 'The *Kulturkampf* was a terrible mistake by Bismarck.' Assess the validity of this statement.

1871–9
Many German Catholics identified with Austria rather than Prussia

1871–8
The National Liberals were the largest party in the *Reichstag*

1871–2
Catholic action against the Old Catholics

1871–9
Catholics made up a third of Germany's population

After 1879 many of the May Laws remained in force

1864
Pope Pius IX's *Syllabus of Errors*

1870
The doctrine of papal infallibility

| 1860 | 1862 | 1864 | 1866 | 1868 | 1870 | 1872 | 1874 | 1876 | 1878 | 1880 |

1871
The formation of the *Kaiserreich*

1871
The Centre Party became the second biggest party in the *Reichstag*

1873
Introduction of the May Laws

1874
The Centre Party increased its support in the *Reichstag*

1878
The National Liberals lost support in the *Reichstag*.

1878
Bismarck feared socialism more than Catholicism

1879
Bismarck repealed some of the anti-Catholic measures

1879
Falk was dismissed

Exam focus

Below are a question, a source and a sample answer. Read all three, including the comments around the answer.

Assess the value of Source 1 as evidence for Bismarck's motivation for supporting the *Kulturkampf* and as evidence for a historian studying the start of the *Kulturkampf*. Explain your answer, using the source, the information given about its origin and your own knowledge about the historical context.

SOURCE 1

Part of an address by Chancellor Otto von Bismarck to the *Reichstag*, 30 January 1872. The *Reichstag* had been elected in 1871. Dominated by the National Liberals (with 125 seats), the *Reichstag* also contained 58 members of the Centre Party, which represented the interests of German Roman Catholics. Bismarck's speech was documented by *Reichstag* officials whose job it was to record all speeches in the German parliament.

When I returned from France, I learned what tactics this new [Centre] party used in order to achieve success in elections. We had hoped that a pious, clerical party would be a prop for the government, would render unto Caesar that which is Caesar's, that it would display respect for the government even when it considered the government mistaken and would maintain a sense of proportion, especially among the masses, in the circles of the common man who knows little about politics. But I was forced to listen in sadness and indignation as election speeches, most of which were also printed, and press articles influenced the elections by appealing in particular to the passions of the lower classes, arousing them against the government ... I never read anything good about the Prussian government, anything acknowledging its achievements, in any of these election speeches ...

The government is determined, and I believe that nobody can honestly doubt this, to see that every confession [religious persuasion] can move freely within this state, especially such a distinguished and numerically large confession as the Catholic. But that it can exercise dominion outside its sphere, that we can never grant, and I believe that this conflict involves areas where the Church hierarchy seeks conquests, not where it is defending itself ...

[Bismarck then criticised a Catholic bishop for disciplining a teacher in the public school system who refused to teach the doctrine of papal infallibility.] The laws of the state forbid us from transferring to a bishop of the Catholic Church the right to discharge a civil servant. Here a collision between canon [Church] law as it has recently developed and the existing laws of the state is unavoidable. This conflict must be skilfully resolved; I regard that as the task of further legislation and I believe that the new minister of culture [Adalbert Falk] will undertake this task with zeal and dispatch. The government has no intention of undertaking dogmatic disputes concerning the changes of declaration that have recently occurred within the realm of Catholic Church dogma; every dogma, even that not believed by us, which is shared by so many millions of fellow countrymen, must be considered sacred by their fellow citizens and the government. But we cannot concede the claim by religious authorities to the permanent exercises of a part of state power, and insofar as they possess a part thereof, we are compelled in the interests of peace to reduce that part ... so that we can live peacefully beside each other, so that we will be able to discuss theology here as little as possible.

Correct

Bismarck's speech to the *Reichstag* on 30 January 1872 is likely to be of considerable value to historians studying Bismarck's motives for supporting the *Kulturkampf* or to historians simply studying the start of the *Kulturkampf*. Clearly the two issues are very much linked. It is likely that a struggle between the (perceived) reactionary Catholic Church and liberals (in Germany and elsewhere) would have occurred with or without Bismarck's intervention. But Bismarck's decision to support the *Kulturkampf* was crucial. The *Kulturkampf* in Germany would have been a very different affair had he not become involved. In the *Reichstag* speech, he explains some of his reasons for his involvement. This speech, in itself, was something of a historical event in that it publicly launched Bismarck's clash with Catholicism. It provides some of his motives for the clash and some reasons why many other Germans were similarly suspicious of the Catholic Church at this time.

This is a strong introduction. It immediately links the two parts of the question. It also shows good awareness of the situation in January 1872.

One of Bismarck's key reasons for involvement in the *Kulturkampf* was the political situation in Germany. In the source extract, Bismarck is critical of the actions of Catholic Centre Party politicians. The Centre Party had been formed in North Germany in 1871 to defend Catholic interests. After the creation of the German Empire in 1871, it joined forces with south Germans. After the elections in 1871 it became the second-largest party in the *Reichstag*. Bismarck bemoans the actions of Centre Party politicians who, in the course of the elections, had had nothing good to say about his government or about Prussia.

This short, incisive paragraph is essentially a paraphrase of part of Bismarck's speech. But it also provides some context with regard to the Centre Party. This is cleverly done.

A second motive was Bismarck's concern about matters of Church and state. In the source Bismarck is critical of the Catholic Church hierarchy for actively seeking to interfere in matters which (in his – and many other Germans' – view) are essentially matters of state. By 1872 the Catholic Church's actions with regard to the so-called Old Catholics had become a matter of concern in Germany. Some 5,000 'Old Catholics' (mainly teachers and lecturers) refused to accept the 1870 Vatican Council decision which supported the doctrine of papal infallibility. This ruled that papal pronouncements on matters of faith and morals could not easily be questioned. In late 1871 Catholic bishops began to dismiss – or threaten to dismiss – Old Catholic teachers and professors. Bismarck saw this as a major source of concern. The Catholic Church, in his view, was interfering in state matters, which had to stop. (Centre Party politicians saw things differently: most objected to state interference in the Church's traditional sphere of influence, the education system.) Bismarck declares that the government will be forced to take action and states that the new Minister of Culture, Adalbert Falk, will introduce relevant legislation 'with zeal and dispatch'. Germans of whatever religious persuasion, Bismarck says, must live peacefully together. Theological concerns should not be a concern of the *Reichstag*.

This is a longer paragraph than the last but displays many of the same skills – ability to paraphrase effectively, clear understanding of the issues, and good awareness of the context which is interwoven into the paraphrasing.

It should be said that this speech, like almost any other by Bismarck, has limitations. When it comes to primary evidence on Bismarck, the problem is not a lack of material but an excess. He left a wealth of letters, articles, speeches and official reports. (Following this speech in the *Reichstag*, he wrote a number of published articles critical of the Catholic Church and in favour of religious toleration.) There were also his Reminiscences, written after he retired and long after the events. Unfortunately, in both his speeches and writings, Bismarck did not always reveal his real intentions or motives. Thus, his own evidence needs to be used with caution. A single letter or speech is not necessarily a true reflection of his policies or intentions at any given time. Moreover, Bismarck was a supreme opportunist – and was proud of his skill on this

A fascinating paragraph which has sensible things to say about the problems associated with almost all of Bismarck's writing and speeches. To what extent did he mean what he said on 30 January 1872? This is a good question to ask because historians are never quite sure!

front. It is thus difficult to disentangle with any certainty his motives, or to decide how far he planned ahead. It may be, for example, that he said what he said on 30 January 1872 for reasons which are not as obvious as they might seem.

What Bismarck does not say in the speech is almost as important as what he does say. Like all politicians, he did not necessarily provide all the reasons for his actions. The new German Empire had been created in 1871 (as a result of the Franco-Prussian War). Four southern German states – Bavaria, Württemberg, Baden and Hesse-Darmstadt – had effectively joined the North German Confederation, dominated by Prussia. Prior to 1870, these Catholic states had looked more to Austria for leadership than Prussia. Part of the reason for this was religion. The four southern states were Catholic (like Austria) whereas Prussia was Protestant. The inhabitants of the south German states were not the only Catholic inhabitants of the new *Kaiserreich*. Catholicism was also strong in the Rhineland, among Prussia's Polish population and in Alsace-Lorraine, annexed from France in 1871. Catholics now comprised a third of the new Germany's population. Bismarck viewed the Catholic minority with suspicion. His greatest concern in domestic policy after 1871 was to unify and consolidate the new Reich. Suspicious of those who opposed his creation, he saw plots and subversive activities everywhere. Bismarck saw the success of the Centre Party in 1871 as a grave danger to the Empire's unity. He feared that Centre politicians would encourage civil disobedience among Catholics whenever the policies of the state conflicted with those of the Church. His suspicions deepened when he observed how rapidly the Centre Party became a rallying point for opponents of the Empire. Bismarck may imply some of this in his speech. But he does not actually say it.

Nor did Bismarck say much about another possible political motivation. The new German constitution, which Bismarck himself had devised, gave the Kaiser and his Chancellor considerable powers. However, the new Germany had some important democratic elements, not least a democratically elected *Reichstag*. While the powers of the *Reichstag* were limited, the body could accept or reject legislation. It could thus embarrass Bismarck. He knew that, politically, he would be much stronger if he could work with the *Reichstag*. After the 1871 elections, the *Reichstag* was dominated by the National Liberals. Bismarck was aware that most National Liberals were fiercely opposed to the Catholic Church, which they saw as a bastion of reaction. Various papal measures in the 1860s, culminating in the Vatican Council laying down the doctrine of papal infallibility, aroused great alarm in German liberal circles. Many of Germany's most enlightened men believed that the Catholic Church's actions meant that the future of mankind was at stake. Bismarck was aware of this. It may be that the *Kulturkampf* was a calculated political ploy on his part to put himself at the head of a popular, Protestant 'crusade'. It certainly enabled him to work closely with the National Liberals for most of the 1870s.

Bismarck may also have had stronger religious motives than the source implies. He was a very sincere Protestant, a fact which historians sometimes also forget. Like many devout Protestants, he had little affection for Catholicism and viewed the recent actions of the papacy with alarm. It may be that he really believed that the anti-Prussian political alignment in the *Reichstag* was a papal-inspired conspiracy of malcontents bent on destroying the Reich. But like almost everything written on Bismarck's motivation, this is debatable.

This paragraph very much links to the last. The first sentence is a very good observation. Bismarck probably had other motivations, not mentioned in the speech. The paragraph examines other possible motives, displaying excellent contextual knowledge in the process.

Another very good paragraph, very much linking back to the previous one, and showing similar contextual awareness.

A short but very effective paragraph. Virtually every sentence has something interesting and important to say.

In conclusion, Bismarck's speech is clearly important with regard to both the start of the *Kulturkampf* and to Bismarck's motives. The clash with the Catholic Church was an important aspect of German politics in the 1870s. Although centred on Prussia (where Falk was particularly important), its effects were felt throughout Germany. Legislation against the Church was passed in Prussia, by other state governments and by the *Reichstag*. The *Kulturkampf* continued throughout most of the 1870s. Its results were not what Bismarck had hoped. Catholic communities remained loyal to their faith and Bismarck's hopes of destroying the Centre Party backfired: the *Kulturkampf* strengthened rather than weakened his political opponents. In 1871 the Centre won 58 seats; in 1874 it won 91. In 1878 Bismarck finally accepted that the *Kulturkampf* had failed and symbolically dismissed Falk in 1879. The fact that the *Kulturkampf* lasted as long as it did, however, suggests that Bismarck was strongly committed to it. The *Reichstag* speech in January 1872 may, therefore, well reflect Bismarck's feelings on the issue more than many of his speeches on other matters.

The conclusion gets off to a somewhat disappointing start. It recaps what happened next rather than summing up what has been said in the essay. However, its last sentence pulls things together with a vengeance, linking future developments to Bismarck's motives in 1872.

This is a clear Level 5 answer. The candidate shows an excellent understanding of the source, its context and Bismarck. The candidate displays ability to analyse the source in a sophisticated way with regard to both lines of enquiry. He/she is able to use his/her contextual knowledge to make a number of important inferences and judgements with relation to the source.

Linking factors

One of the reasons why this essay is so successful is that it draws links between the factors it discusses. Read through the essay again and highlight the points at which the factors are linked.

2 The birth of democratic Germany, 1917–19

The strains of war, tensions and military dictatorship, 1917

REVISED

The situation, 1914–16

In 1914 Germany, allied with Austria–Hungary (and later Turkey and Bulgaria), went to war with the Allies – Britain, France, Serbia and Russia (and later Italy, Romania and the USA). Despite Germany's failure to secure a quick victory, dissident views were few in 1914–15. Germans remained united against the perceived threat posed by 'barbaric' Russia. Lulled into a false sense of security by official propaganda, most remained hopeful of victory. Until mid-1916, Chancellor Bethmann-Hollweg faced little opposition from the public or the *Reichstag*.

Military interference

As the war progressed, Germany's military leaders interfered increasingly in political and economic affairs, justifying their actions on the grounds of military necessity. Wilhelm II, who had ruled as well as reigned in Germany after Bismarck's fall in 1890, exerted little control. His self-confidence seemed to desert him with the onset of war. Despite being supreme warlord, he was kept in the dark about military developments and his advice was rarely sought. He thus became little more than a figurehead.

Financial and economic problems

- Germany had a huge financial deficit pre-1914 and once war started it soared. Bethmann-Hollweg's government, rather than raise taxes, simply printed money. This fuelled inflation.
- The British naval blockade, poor harvests, problems of transportation, shortage of chemicals for fertilisers, and mass conscription led to a serious decline in agricultural production. By 1916 virtually every foodstuff was rationed.

The roles of Hindenburg and Ludendorff

In 1916 Bethmann-Hollweg ditched General Falkenhayn, Chief of the Army Supreme Command. Field Marshal **Paul von Hindenburg** and General Erich Ludendorff, two officers who had won important victories against Russia, were appointed Chief of the General Staff and Quartermaster-General respectively, and given joint responsibility for the conduct of military operations. Far from strengthening his position, Bethmann-Hollweg soon found that his and Wilhelm's authority had been weakened, since neither of them enjoyed Hindenburg and Ludendorff's popularity. By simply threatening to resign, the two warlords exerted a powerful influence over events – political, economic and military. Their 'rule' is often described as 'the silent dictatorship'.

Mobilisation of resources

Hindenburg and Ludendorff tried to mobilise German resources more thoroughly than before. For example:

- Ludendorff ordered the systematic exploitation of enemy areas occupied by German troops.
- The Auxiliary Service Act (December 1916) enabled the government to control the labour of all males between 17 and 60.
- A Supreme War Office was set up and given wide powers over industry and labour.

The threat of defeat

By 1917 Hindenburg and Ludendorff, fearing that Germany faced defeat, believed that they had no option but to take greater risks. It could be that this risk-taking actually brought about the defeat that Germany's 'silent dictators' were trying to avert. The introduction of unrestricted submarine warfare, for example, brought the USA into the war against Germany in April 1917.

Civilian morale

On the domestic front the war's impact remorselessly affected the lives of ordinary Germans, weakening morale. Shortages of food and fuel made life, for most, truly miserable. Civilian deaths from starvation and hypothermia increased from 121,000 in 1916 to 293,000 in 1918. Many workers resented being forced to work even longer hours as a result of the Auxiliary Service Law. Social discontent grew markedly. By 1917–18 the 'left' organised an increasing number of strikes. The 'right' blamed Jews and socialists for all Germany's problems.

You're the examiner

Below are a sample exam question and a paragraph written in answer to the question. Read the paragraph and the mark schemes provided on page 111. Describe what level you would award the paragraph. Write the level below along with a justification for your choice.

To what extent was Germany a military dictatorship by 1917?

> In August 1916 Field Marshal Hindenburg and General Ludendorff were appointed joint Chiefs of the Army Supreme Command. The two men had won important victories on the Eastern Front. They were thus far more popular than Chancellor Bethmann-Hollweg or Kaiser Wilhelm II. By simply threatening to resign, Hindenburg and Ludendorff exerted a huge influence over not just the army but political and economic matters as well. The two men remained in power until September 1918. Their 'rule' is often described as 'the silent dictatorship'. However, powerful though they were, they did not have total control of Germany.

Level:

Mark:

☐   ☐

Reason for choosing this level and this mark:

_____

_____

Develop the detail **a**

Below are a sample exam-style question and a paragraph written in answer to this question. The paragraph contains a limited amount of detail. Annotate the paragraph to add additional detail to the answer.

How accurate is it to say that Germany was on the verge of defeat in 1917?

> By 1917 Germany faced major economic problems. The country was short of food. Life for most Germans was truly miserable. This meant that there was growing discontent among civilians. In many ways Germany's internal problems were as serious as its military problems.

Political crisis, 1917

The July 1917 crisis

As disillusionment with the conduct of the war increased, so did dissent in the *Reichstag*. Bethmann-Hollweg, hoping to maintain unity, persuaded Wilhelm to promise reform of the Prussian franchise system, to conservative alarm.

War aims

The issue of war aims divided Germans.
- Right-wing parties sought territorial acquisitions, ensuring German dominance over Europe.
- Left-wing parties believed that Germany was fighting a defensive war, not one of conquest. Thus any peace settlement was to be based upon reconciliation with no territorial annexations.

Bethmann-Hollweg did his best to avoid debate on war aims. However, by mid-1917 it was impossible to overlook the rift between those who sought a 'peace without victory' and those who supported a 'victorious peace'. In June 1917 left-wing parties made it clear that they would vote against war credits if Bethmann-Hollweg did not support 'peace without victory'. He refused, thus losing the support of the *Reichstag*.

On 6 July:
- Matthias Erzberger, a Centre politician, called upon the *Reichstag* to pass a 'peace without victory' resolution.
- The main political parties established a Joint Committee to consider constitutional reform.

Bethmann-Hollweg's resignation

Ludendorff, no longer prepared to work with a man who supported political change and who had lost control of the *Reichstag*, forced Bethmann-Hollweg to resign in July. Georg Michaelis, an insignificant administrator, became Chancellor. He was the tool of Hindenburg and Ludendorff.

Erzberger's peace resolution

On 19 July, Erzberger's peace resolution passed the *Reichstag* by 212 votes to 126. Michaelis assured Germans that he would respect the resolution 'as I interpret it'. Satisfied that they had won a significant victory, the majority parties voted for the war credits. However, Erzberger's resolution had no influence on Germany's military leaders, who remained committed to winning a victorious peace.

Other developments

The emergence of the Independent Socialist Party

By 1917 German socialists were seriously divided. Most SPD deputies, unwilling to damage the war effort, were prepared to work with the other parties. However, a number of radicals opposed collaboration with the capitalist German state. In April 1917, 42 SPD deputies formed a new party, the Independent Social Democratic Party (USPD). The remaining 68 SPD deputies reconstituted themselves as the Majority Socialists with **Friedrich Ebert** as chairman.

The USPD was loosely associated with:
- the Spartacus League, a group of socialist intellectuals, led by Karl Liebknecht and **Rosa Luxemburg**
- the **revolutionary shop stewards**, who unlike the Spartacists had considerable grass roots influence.

The Spartacus League and the shop stewards, inspired by the 1917 Russian revolutions, believed that working people must destroy capitalism and begin a process of world revolution.

Right-wing reaction

Nationalists, alarmed by the peace resolution, founded the Fatherland Party in September 1917. Heavily subsidised by industrialists, the Party demanded annexations and supported military rule. It soon claimed to have over one million members. (It probably had fewer than 500,000.)

Chancellor Hertling

In November 1917 Michaelis was dismissed for his inept handling of a small naval mutiny. The *Reichstag* played a key role in his dismissal but not in his replacement. Wilhelm II chose Count Hertling, an elderly aristocrat. Hertling, while disliking parliamentary government, promised to support the peace resolution and to reform the Prussian franchise. Ludendorff, busy with preparations for the 1918 offensive, hoped that Hertling's conciliatory measures would keep the home front quiet long enough for Germany to win the war.

Mind map

Use the information on the opposite page to add detail to the mind map below. This information should help you understand the importance of the July 1917 crisis.

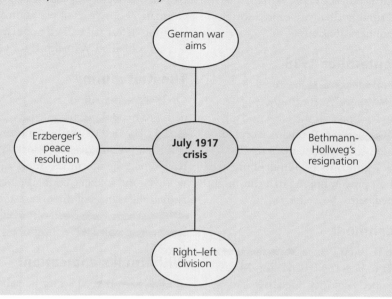

 Introducing an argument

Below are a sample exam-style question, a list of key points to be made in the essay, and a simple introduction and conclusion for the essay. Read the question, the plan and the introduction and conclusion. Rewrite the introduction and the conclusion in order to develop an argument.

To what extent did the events of July 1917 amount to a serious political crisis?

Key points

- Divisions between right and left
- Bethmann-Hollweg's resignation
- Erzberger's peace resolution
- The end of the crisis?

Introduction

In July 1917 it was clear that Germans were politically divided – left against right. This division led to a major crisis.

Conclusion

The July 1917 'crisis' thus ended without too much change. But the political divisions which had caused the crisis remained. Indeed, right and left were even more bitterly divided.

Constitutional reforms from above, 1918

The role of Prince Max von Baden

By 1918 four years of war had dislocated Germany's economy, wrecked government finances, caused social tensions and increased political divisions.

The situation in September 1918

On 29 September General Ludendorff informed Wilhelm II that the war was lost. Accordingly, Chancellor Hertling was to approach the USA and ask for an armistice. On 30 September Wilhelm accepted Hertling's resignation and issued a proclamation establishing parliamentary government. Hindenburg and Ludendorff abdicated their power, hoping that this might ensure Germany obtained better peace terms.

Prince Max's government

On 1 October Wilhelm II asked Prince Max von Baden, a moderate conservative, to become Chancellor. Max's government, which included Majority Socialists, had little option but to ask US President Wilson for an armistice. Several weeks of secret negotiation followed.

Constitutional reform

Max's government introduced a series of constitutional reforms that turned Germany into a parliamentary monarchy:
- Prussia's three-class franchise was abolished.
- The Kaiser's military powers were curtailed.
- The Chancellor and the government were made accountable to the *Reichstag*.

Most Germans paid little heed to the hugely important reforms. After all, Wilhelm remained Kaiser, a prince was Chancellor, and the war continued. Nor did the *Reichstag* behave as if the changes represented a major turning point. It adjourned on 5 October, did not meet until 22 October, and then adjourned again until 9 November.

Revolution from above?

The constitutional changes were essentially a 'revolution from above'. Nevertheless, much of what occurred resulted from the *Reichstag*'s influence. In September 1918 a *Reichstag* committee had called for the creation of a government responsible to the *Reichstag*. While parliamentary government came into being largely by order of the Supreme Command, it is therefore unlikely that *Reichstag* pressure for political change could have been resisted for much longer.

The revolutionary situation

By late October a revolutionary situation existed in Germany. Four years of privation and the shock of looming defeat radicalised popular attitudes. Most Germans blamed Wilhelm II for Germany's misfortunes.

The Kiel mutiny

On 29 October rumours that the High Seas Fleet was going to be sent out on a do-or-die mission against the Royal Navy led to a sailors' mutiny at Wilhelmshaven and Kiel. On 4 November dockworkers and soldiers in Kiel joined the mutinous sailors and set up Russian-style workers' and soldiers' councils. News of events in Kiel fanned the flames of discontent across Germany. By 8 November revolutionary councils, demanding peace, had been established in most cities.

Wilhelm II's abdication

On 7 November, Majority Socialist leaders threatened to withdraw support from the government unless Wilhelm abdicated and socialists were given greater representation. When Max failed to persuade Wilhelm to abdicate, Majority Socialist ministers Philipp Scheidemann and Gustav Bauer resigned and the Party called a general strike.

On 9 November, with most workers on strike and troops in Berlin unreliable, Max announced Wilhelm's abdication. Lacking support from his generals, Wilhelm fled to the Netherlands. Max also resigned, handing over power to Friedrich Ebert.

On 11 November Ebert's new republican government agreed to Allied armistice terms. The First World War, in which over 2 million Germans had died, ended.

Complete the paragraph

Below are a sample exam-style question and a paragraph written in answer to this question. The paragraph contains a point and specific examples, but lacks a concluding explanatory link back to the question. Complete the paragraph, adding this link in the space provided.

To what extent did the events in Germany between 29 September and 11 November 1918 amount to a revolution?

> In early November the revolutionary situation in Germany gathered momentum. On 7 November Majority Socialist leaders threatened to withdraw support from the government unless Wilhelm abdicated and socialists were given greater representation in the cabinet. When Prince Max failed to persuade Wilhelm to abdicate, the Majority Socialist ministers Scheidemann and Bauer resigned. The Majority Socialists now agreed to support a general strike on 9 November. By 9 November virtually all Germany's army leaders realised that the Kaiser had to go. Abandoned by his generals, Wilhelm accepted the reality of the situation and fled to the Netherlands. Prince Max resigned and a new government, led by the Majority Socialist leader Ebert, came to power.
>
> _____
>
> _____

Spectrum of significance

Below are a sample exam-style question and a list of general points which could be used to answer the question. Use your own knowledge and the information in this section to reach a judgement about the importance of these general points to the question posed. Write numbers on the spectrum below to indicate their relative importance. Having done this, write a brief justification of your placement, explaining why some of these factors are more important than others. The resulting diagram could form the basis of an essay plan.

How far did events in Germany between 29 September and 11 November 1918 amount to a revolution?

1 The resignation of Chancellor Hertling

2 Wilhelm II's proclamation establishing parliamentary government

3 The abdication of power by Hindenburg and Ludendorff

4 Prince Max's constitutional reforms

5 The situation in Germany in October 1918

6 The Kiel mutiny

7 The establishment of workers' and soldiers' councils

8 Wilhelm II's abdication

← _____ →

Less important   **More important**

The German Revolution, 1918–19

The revolutionary situation

In November 1918 it seemed that Germany might follow Russia down the path of Communist revolution. Socialists controlled the *Reichstag* and socialist-controlled **soviets** assumed power in many towns.

Divisions among the revolutionaries

German socialists were far from united.

- Majority Socialists upheld parliamentary democracy and rejected Russian-style communism.
- Spartacists and revolutionary shop stewards wanted a socialist republic, based on the workers' and soldiers' councils, which would smash the institutions of imperial Germany.
- Independent Socialists (USPD) demanded radical social and economic change – the nationalisation of key industries, the breaking-up of landed estates and the democratisation of the civil service, the judiciary and the army – to complement political reform.

Ebert's actions

Ebert's position was weak. His government's authority was not even accepted in all parts of Berlin. To increase his support, he offered the USPD seats in the government. The USPD decided (by 21 votes to 19) to accept Ebert's offer. The new government consisted of three SPD and three USPD members. Ebert and Hugo Haase acted as co-chairmen.

Ebert's position

Relations between the Majority Socialists and Independents remained tense. Nevertheless, Ebert's position soon grew stronger.

- On 10 November General Groener agreed that the army would support the government in return for Ebert's promise to preserve the officers' authority.
- On 15 November the Stinnes–Legien agreement did much to satisfy workers' grievances. The trade unions agreed not to interfere with private ownership. In return, employers guaranteed legal recognition to trade unions, agreed to workers' councils, and accepted an eight-hour working day.
- An all-German Congress of Workers' and Soldiers' Councils met in Berlin in mid-December. Most delegates supported the Majority Socialists and approved the government's decision to hold elections to a National Assembly in January 1919.
- On 29 December the Independents resigned from the government. Ebert now had a freer hand.

Revolution?

The Spartacist rising

On 1 January 1919, the Spartacists founded the German Communist Party. Led by Karl Liebknecht and Rosa Luxemburg, the Communists called for government by workers' and soldiers' councils. On 6 January Communist leaders issued a proclamation deposing Ebert. As armed Communists occupied public buildings in Berlin, Ebert's government turned to the army. General Groener, in addition to using regular units, recruited hundreds of right-wing ex-soldiers (*Freikorps*). By mid-January the Spartacist revolt was crushed. Liebknecht and Luxemburg were shot while in police custody.

Further bloodshed

- In March, the Communists called a general strike. Again Berlin became the scene of fighting; again the *Freikorps* restored order at the cost of over 1,000 dead.
- In April, the army and *Freikorps* put down a Communist rebellion in Bavaria.

What revolution?

By April 1919 the revolution had run its course. Whether the events of 1918–19 amounted to a revolution remains debatable. The deposition of the Kaiser and the introduction of parliamentary democracy were important changes. However, the civil service, judiciary and army all remained essentially intact. Nor was there any major change in the structure of big business, land ownership and society.

Ebert has been accused of betraying workers' interests. But he had no wish to preside over chaos. Like most Majority Socialists, he feared the extreme left and thus had little option but to rely on the army. His main concern was to establish a system of parliamentary democracy.

Qualify your judgement

Below is a sample exam question with the accompanying source.

> Assess the value of Source 1 as evidence for a historian investigating the situation in Germany over the winter of 1918–19 and for revealing the aims of German socialists in December 1918. Explain your answer, using the source, the information given about its origin and your own knowledge about the historical context.

Having read the question and source, circle the judgement that best describes the value of the source and explain why it is the best.

1 Source 1 is valuable to a historian because it provides details of the policy of the German government at the end of December 1918.

2 Source 1 is not very valuable to historians because it actually says very little about the situation in Germany over the winter of 1918–19.

3 Source 3 is particularly valuable because it provides information about the concerns of Ebert's SPD government in late December 1918 and what measures it hoped would appeal to the German people.

SOURCE 1

This declaration of the programme of the SPD was issued on 29 December 1918, the same day that the three Independent Socialists left the German government. The resignation of the Independent Socialists left the Majority Socialists, led by Friedrich Ebert, in control of a government which faced a number of crises. The declaration, rushed out by the government, was an attempt to inform the German people of its intentions.

To the German people!

Workers! Soldiers! Citizens! Citizenesses!

The Independents have left the government. The remaining members of the Cabinet vacated their posts so that the Central Council could have a wholly free hand. The latter unanimously re-instated them. The crippling disunity is at an end. The Reich government is reconstructed and united. It professes but one principle: the well being, the survival, the indivisibility of the German Republic above all party interest. On the unanimous recommendation of the Central Council two members of the Social Democratic Party, Noske and Wissell, have replaced the three Independents who resigned. All Cabinet members are equal. Chairmen are Ebert and Scheidemann. And now for our programme. At home:

– to prepare for the National Assembly, urgently attend to feeding [the people], initiate socialisation … deal severely with war profiteering, create jobs and support the unemployed, improve dependants' relief, to develop the people's army with all means and to disarm unauthorised [personnel].

Abroad

– to achieve peace as quickly and as favourably as possible and to re-staff the foreign representations of the German Republic with men imbued with the new spirit.

That is the broad outline of our programme prior to the National Assembly.

It will be effected in close contact with the German free states. Its execution will be evident not in words but in deeds. Now we will have the opportunity to act! It would be our fault alone if we failed to avail ourselves of it! We must set to! But you must work with us! The new Republic belongs to all of us. Help to secure it! The question raised by the Central Council is also directed at you:

'Are you able to defend peace and order against violent attacks and to guarantee the Government's work with all means available against violence, no matter from which side it is perpetrated?'

You must answer this question with a *Yes!* The government has done so without qualification. Without this Yes! the programme will remain paper and words! We want to go beyond appeals to action! We are getting down to work! We believe in you and in ourselves. We will win through!

The government of the Reich: Ebert, Scheidemann, Landsberg, Noske, Wissell.

The attempt to achieve unity through democracy: the Weimar Republic

REVISED

The 1919 elections

Having survived the left-wing threat in 1918–19, Ebert's government pushed ahead with plans to establish a new constitution.

The political parties

Elections for the National Assembly took place on 19 January 1919. Most political parties took the opportunity to re-form themselves. New names did not hide the fact that there was considerable continuity in the party system's structure.

- The Nationalist Party (DNVP) was essentially an amalgamation of the old Conservative parties.
- The liberals remained divided between left (the Democrats) and right (the People's Party).
- The Majority Socialists now called themselves the SPD.

The election results

The results were a success for the forces of parliamentary democracy. Over 80 per cent of the electorate (including women) voted. The SPD won 165 seats (38 per cent of the vote), the Centre 91 seats, the Democrats 75, the Nationalists 44, the SDPD 22 and the People's Party 19. The election, a clear repudiation of the extreme right and left, seemed a promising start to a new chapter in German history.

The Weimar Coalition

In February 1919 the National Assembly met at Weimar; Berlin was considered unsafe because of the Communist threat. Ebert was elected the Republic's first President by 277 votes to 51. He asked the SPD to form a government. The SPD found allies in the Centre and Democrat parties – the so-called 'Weimar Coalition'. Over 75 per cent of the electorate had voted for these three parties, all of which were committed to parliamentary democracy. The new government, headed by Scheidemann, consisted of six Social Democrats, three Centrists and three Democrats.

The Weimar constitution

The Assembly's main task was to draw up a new constitution. That constitution was passed by the National Assembly by 262 votes to 75 on 31 July 1919. Only the USPD and far right parties opposed it.

The main principles

- Germany was to be a republic, its sovereignty based on the people.
- It remained a federal rather than a unitary state, comprising 18 states (or *Länder*).
- At national level Germany was to be governed by a *Reichstag*, a *Reichsrat* and a President.
- The central government would control direct taxation, foreign affairs, the armed forces and communications.
- *Länder* retained their powers over education, police and the Churches.
- A Bill of Rights guaranteed personal liberty, equality before the law, freedom of movement, expression and conscience and freedom to belong to a trade union.

The *Reichstag*

Reichstag deputies were to be elected every four years by all Germans over the age of 20. A system of proportional representation was introduced, ensuring that the *Reichstag* would represent all views. The Chancellor and his ministers had to possess the *Reichstag*'s confidence and were obliged to resign when they forfeited it. The *Reichstag* was to initiate and approve legislation.

The *Reichsrat*

The *Reichsrat* was composed of delegates from the *Länder*. Each *Land* was represented according to its population, except that none was allowed to have more than two-fifths of the seats (to prevent Prussian preponderance). The *Reichsrat* could veto *Reichstag* legislation, but its veto could be over-ridden by a two-thirds vote of the *Reichstag*.

The President

The President, elected by the people for seven years, was supreme commander of the armed forces, convened and dissolved the *Reichstag*, could block new laws by calling a referendum, and appointed the Chancellor and the federal government.

! Spot the mistake a

Below are a sample exam-style question and an introductory paragraph written in answer to this question. Why does this paragraph not get into Level 4? Once you have identified the mistake, rewrite the paragraph so that it displays the qualities of Level 4. The mark scheme on page 111 will help you.

> 'The Weimar constitution was a triumph for democracy in 1919.' Explain why you agree or disagree with this view.

> Over the winter of 1918–19, it seemed that Germany might follow Russia down the path of Communist dictatorship. This did not happen. Instead, in January 1919 an elected National Assembly met in Weimar to agree to a new constitution. This constitution was probably the most democratic constitution in Europe.

⬥ Develop the detail a

Below are a sample exam-style question and the paragraph written in answer to this question from the activity above. The paragraph contains a limited amount of detail. Annotate the paragraph to add additional detail to the answer.

> 'The Weimar constitution was a triumph for Friedrich Ebert in 1919.' Assess the validity of this view.

> Following elections a National Assembly met in Weimar to agree to a new constitution. The largest party in the Assembly was the SPD. SPD leader Ebert was elected as President. But this was not a total triumph for Ebert. Lacking an overall majority, the SPD had to co-operate with other pro-democracy parties.

The importance of the Weimar constitution

The weaknesses of the constitution

For historians looking for structural reasons to explain the Republic's eventual collapse in 1933, it is easy to claim that the 1919 constitution was a major source of weakness.

The problem of proportional representation

The introduction of proportional representation is usually seen as a major problem for the fledgling Republic. This system of voting encouraged the formation of new parties, usually representing particular interests. The fact that there were so many parties ensured no political party was ever likely to win an overall majority in the *Reichstag*. This led to coalition governments, which came and went with spectacular frequency after 1919. Such instability meant there was weak government.

The presidency

The creation of a presidency, intended to act as a counter-balance to the *Reichstag*, created a somewhat ambiguous system. Was the ultimate source of authority in the Republic vested in the *Reichstag* or the presidency? The situation was further exacerbated by the powers conferred on the President by Article 48. This provided the President with the authority to suspend civil rights and to take whatever action was required to restore law and order by the issue of presidential decrees. Although the intention was to create the means by which government could continue to function in a temporary crisis, Article 48 gave the President considerable potential power.

The strengths of the constitution

Arguably there was nothing structurally wrong with the 1919 constitution. It reflected both a broad spectrum of political opinion and successful constitutional practice at the time.

A democratic system

The Weimar constitution was thoroughly democratic. It also tried to build on Germany's traditional practices. In recognising an element of regional authority (for example, over the police) and regional influence, such as representation of the *Länder* in the *Reichsrat*, the constitution reflected pre-1914 practice.

Was proportional representation a weakness?

Although there had been no proportional representation system before 1919, there had been a large number of political parties. Parties in pre-1914 Germany had usually represented sectional – usually class – interests. None of those parties ever won overall majorities in the *Reichstag*. Parties were used to forming coalitions. This was the way German politics operated. Proportional representation ensured that a wide variety of interests were represented in the *Reichstag*. The abundance of small parties did not necessarily mean weak government. The fundamental problem was the large parties' difficulty in creating coalitions and agreeing policies.

Presidential power

Presidential powers were limited. Article 48 allowed government sufficient flexibility to overcome serious problems facing the Republic between 1919 and 1923.

Freedom and civil liberties

The Weimar constitution passed a Bill of Rights which guaranteed German people personal liberty, equality before the law, freedom of movement, expression and conscience and freedom to belong to a trade union.

The situation in 1919

Arguably, by providing an essentially liberal democratic framework, the 1919 constitution represented a major improvement on the far more authoritarian 1871 constitution. Unfortunately, the Weimar constitution could not control the conditions and circumstances in which it had to operate. No constitution could have provided for all the possible consequences arising from the immense problems Germany faced following its defeat in 1918. These problems included:

- making peace with the Allied powers
- dealing with the terrible economic and financial legacy of the First World War
- resisting the Communist threat
- resisting the threat from nationalist and anti-Semitic groups on the extreme right who blamed Weimar politicians for Germany's defeat in the war.

Support or challenge?

Below is a sample exam-style question which asks how far you agree with a specific statement. Below this is a series of general statements which are relevant to the question. Using your own knowledge and the information on the opposite page, decide whether these statements support or challenge the statement in the question and tick the appropriate box.

'There was little wrong with the Weimar constitution in theory.' How far do you agree with this view?

	SUPPORT	CHALLENGE
The Weimar constitution was far more democratic than the 1871 constitution.		
The Weimar constitution introduced proportional representation.		
Proportional representation encouraged the formation of many political parties.		
Proportional representation ensured that most people's views were represented in the *Reichstag*.		
The Weimar constitution resulted in unstable coalition government.		
The Weimar President could rule by decree.		
The Weimar President was elected democratically.		
The Weimar constitution guaranteed a wide range of civil liberties.		
The Weimar constitution established a federal system of government.		

 Simple essay style

Below is a sample exam-style question. Use your own knowledge and the information on the opposite page to produce a plan for this question. Choose four general points and provide three pieces of specific information to support each general point. Once you have planned the essay, write the introduction and conclusion for the essay. The introduction should list the points to be discussed in the essay. The conclusion should summarise the key points and justify which point was the most important.

To what extent was the Weimar constitution flawed?

Exam focus

Below is a sample essay. Read it and the comments around it.

To what extent did events in Germany between September 1918 and January 1919 amount to a revolution?

The events in Germany between September 1918 and January 1919 are often referred to as a 'German Revolution'. In reality, there were several different mini-revolutions, each with its own aims and agendas. The result was considerable political change. In September 1918 Germany was ruled by the 1871 constitution, a constitution which left great power in the hands of the Kaiser. By January 1919, that constitution had been overthrown, Kaiser Wilhelm II had abdicated and Germany had elected a National Assembly to draw up a democratic constitution. These were major political changes. However, they did not lead to a social revolution as many on the extreme left had hoped. Germany did not go the way of Russia. Whether the political changes in themselves amounted to a revolution is a moot point.

By late September 1918 Germany was on the point of defeat in the First World War, a war which had dislocated Germany's economy, caused serious social tensions and exacerbated the polarisation of politics. On 29 September General Ludendorff, one of Germany's 'silent' military dictators, informed Wilhelm and Chancellor Hertling that the war was lost and that Germany should ask the USA for an armistice. The following day, Wilhelm accepted Hertling's resignation and issued a proclamation establishing parliamentary government. Hindenburg and Ludendorff abdicated their power, leaving the *Reichstag* in control. These events, the first of several major political changes, scarcely amounted to a revolution.

On 1 October Wilhelm asked Prince Max von Baden, a moderate conservative, to form a government. His new government, which included representatives from the Majority Socialists and the Left Liberals, began peace negotiations with the USA. It also introduced a series of constitutional reforms that turned Germany into a parliamentary monarchy. The three-class franchise was abolished in Prussia, the Kaiser's powers over the military were curtailed, and the Chancellor and the government were made accountable to the *Reichstag*. Oddly, most Germans paid little heed to the (ill-publicised) reforms. After all, Wilhelm remained Kaiser, a prince was still Chancellor and the war continued. Nor did the *Reichstag* behave as if the changes represented a turning point in German history. Adjourning on 5 October, it did not meet until 22 October when it again adjourned until 9 November. But Max's constitutional changes, the so-called 'revolution from above', were hugely important.

By late October a revolutionary situation existed in Germany. Four years of privation had eroded the old relationship between ruler and subject, while the shock of looming defeat radicalised popular attitudes. Many Germans saw Wilhelm II as an obstacle of peace and there were calls for his abdication. At the end of October sailors of the German High Seas Fleet mutinied at Wilhelmshaven. The mutiny, essentially a spontaneous protest movement, not a politically led event, rapidly spread to Kiel and other ports. On 4 November dockworkers and soldiers in Kiel joined the mutinous sailors and set up workers' and soldiers' councils on the 1917 Russian model. News of events in Kiel fanned the flames of discontent across Germany. By 8 November revolutionary councils had been established in most major cities. The councils demanded peace and assumed control of local food supplies and services. In Bavaria, the Wittelsbach dynasty was deposed and an independent socialist republic was proclaimed. Extreme left-wing socialists, especially Spartacists and revolutionary shop stewards, campaigned for a socialist republic based on the revolutionary councils, which would smash the institutions of imperial Germany and lead to the nationalisation of key industries,

This is a confident and well-informed introduction, very much linked to the set question. It paves the way for what is likely to follow.

This paragraph examines, quite succinctly, the situation in September 1918. It shows detailed knowledge (of dates, names and events) and the last sentence links back to the question.

Another excellent, well-written paragraph which continues to focus on the set question. The last sentence is an important one.

This is a meaty, important paragraph. It makes the vital point that a revolutionary situation existed in Germany – and shows why that was. The paragraph is well informed throughout.

the breaking-up of landed estates and the democratisation of the army, the civil service and the judiciary. Strikes and demonstrations by workers were organised. The situation appeared menacing to many Germans, alarmed by what they perceived as 'Russian solutions' being put forward for German problems.

On 9 November, Wilhelm II, lacking the support of his leading generals, abdicated and fled to the Netherlands. Prince Max resigned. A new government, led by the Majority Socialist leader Ebert, took over. Ebert was totally opposed to any kind of Bolshevik revolution. He wanted peace. He also hoped to call elections as soon as possible for a National Assembly which would draw up a new constitution. Ebert agreed to Allied armistice terms on 11 November. His main problem, however, was retaining power in Germany. His authority was threatened by the actions of the Spartacists and revolutionary shop stewards who planned to set up a provisional government based on the revolutionary councils. By allying with the Independent Socialists (for a few crucial weeks) and winning the support of army leader General Groener, Ebert clung to power. He was helped by the fact that an all-German Congress of Workers' and Soldiers' Councils, which met in Berlin from 16 to 21 December, was dominated by Majority Socialists, who approved Ebert's decision to hold elections to a National Assembly on 19 January 1919. The revolution, which extreme left-wing socialists hoped for, seemed on hold.

> A concise paragraph with a clear analytical link to the question. The paragraph is full of relevant detail and the last sentence is again effective.

Ebert was unable to avert a Communist revolution in Berlin in early January 1919. This rising, led by Karl Liebknecht and Rosa Luxemburg, was brutally crushed by the army and by *Freikorps* units – ex-soldiers who loathed socialism. The elections for the National Assembly were thus able to go ahead on 19 January. Over 75 per cent of the electorate voted for the Majority Socialists (now called the SPD) and the Centre and Democrat parties, which were all committed to parliamentary democracy. They formed a broad coalition and began work on drawing up a new constitution. Left-wing aspirations of a major social revolution had been defeated.

> This paragraph, like the last, displays really good understanding of the situation and connects with the question.

Thus, by spring 1919 the German revolution had run its course. The Kaiser and the German princes had been deposed and parliamentary democracy was on its way. These were important changes. However, in the event, the German revolution did not go much further than Max's October 1918 reforms. German society was left almost untouched by events. The civil service, judiciary and army all remained essentially intact and there were no major changes in the structure of big business and land ownership. Serious doubts must remain, therefore, about the nature and extent of the changes that had occurred. There had certainly been a revolutionary situation in Germany. But, unlike in Russia, extreme left-wing revolutionaries had failed to take advantage of the situation. A revolution with a small 'r' rather than a capital 'R' might be the best way of describing the outcome of events.

> The conclusion does what every good conclusion should do. It pulls together the argument that was initiated in the introduction and developed throughout the essay. It presents a thoroughly consistent argument and ends with a fine last sentence.

This is a Level 5 essay due to the fact that it engages with the question and has a clear, balanced and carefully reasoned argument that is sustained throughout. The answer is very well written and covers most of the key areas, of which it shows excellent understanding.

Reverse engineering

The best essays are based on careful plans. Read the essay and the comments and try to work out the general points of the plan used to write the essay. Once you have done this, note down the specific examples used to support each general point.

3 A new Reich, 1933–35

Gleichschaltung, 1933–34

REVISED

The Nazis come to power

Adolf Hitler leader of the National Socialist German Workers' (or Nazi) Party, became Chancellor on 30 January 1933.

Hitler's opportunism

Hitler became Chancellor as a result of the support of President Hindenburg and a deal with Hugenberg, leader of the Nationalist Party (DNVP) and von Papen (a previous Chancellor). Hugenberg and Papen, confident they could control Hitler, underestimated him. Within six months, he had made himself dictator. Historians debate whether this occurred almost by accident or whether it was all part of a master plan. Most likely Hitler had clear ideas about where he wanted to go in 1933 but was not altogether sure how to reach his destination. His first move was certainly planned. Against Hugenberg's wishes, he called for new elections.

The March 1933 election

- The Nazis now had sufficient funds to mount an impressive election campaign.
- Hermann Goering, new Interior Minister of Prussia, recruited 50,000 SA as special police, ensuring that the Nazis could terrorise their opponents legally.
- On 27 February the *Reichstag* was burned down. Van der Lubbe, a Dutch Communist, admitted starting the fire. The Nazis claimed that the fire was a Communist plot – a signal to spark revolution. The Communists blamed the Nazis, claiming that the fire provided Hitler with an excuse to move against the Communists. The fire was certainly convenient for him.
- Hindenburg, convinced that Communists were involved, issued a decree suspending freedom of the press, speech and association.
- Leading Communists and SPD members were arrested.

On 5 March 1933 the Nazis won 43.9 per cent of the vote. The DNVP won 8 per cent. Between them the two parties had a majority.

Hitler's consolidation of power

Hitler moved to enlarge his powers – *Gleichschaltung*

The Enabling Act

To change the constitution, Hitler needed a two-thirds majority. He obtained this by preventing 81 Communist members taking their *Reichstag* seats and by winning Centre Party support. He was thus able to pass the Enabling Act (by 441 votes to 94) in late March. This allowed him to pass laws without the *Reichstag*'s consent.

'Legal revolution'

Hindenburg's *Reichstag* Fire Decree and the Enabling Act gave a veneer of legality to Nazi actions. They described their consolidation of power as a 'legal revolution'.

'Bringing into line'

Hitler quickly 'brought into line' those parts of the political system that were anti-Nazi.

- In April 1933 a law removed Jews and Nazi opponents from the civil service, schools and courts.
- In May 1933 trade unions were abolished.
- In late May 1933 the Nazis occupied SPD and Communist Party offices, confiscating their funds.
- Left-wing newspapers were banned.
- Thousands of Nazi opponents were arrested and placed in concentration camps.
- In June/July 1933 the other political parties dissolved themselves. Germany became officially a one-party state.

The 'co-ordination' of regional and local government

In January 1934 the Law for the Reconstruction of the State dissolved all state assemblies. Germany was now divided into approximately 30 *Gaue*. Each *Gau* was headed by a Nazi-appointed *Gauleiter* (district leader). The Nazis thus ensured that regional and local government policies corresponded with central policies.

The establishment of the DAF

In May 1933 the Nazis established the German Labour Front (DAF: *Deutsche Arbeitsfront*). Led by Robert Ley, its key aims were to reconcile German workers to the Nazi Party by protecting their interests. The DAF set up two subsidiary organisations:

- Strength through Joy: this helped organise workers' leisure time.
- Beauty of Labour: this improved working conditions.

The DAF became the biggest organisation in the Third Reich with a membership of 22 million.

! Complete the paragraph

Below are a sample exam-style question and a paragraph written in answer to this question. The paragraph contains a point and a concluding explanatory link back to the question, but lacks examples. Complete the paragraph, adding examples in the space provided.

'Nazi consolidation of power in 1933–34 was achieved legally and with relatively little violence.' How far do you agree with this statement about *Gleichschaltung*?

In March 1933 the *Reichstag* passed the Enabling Act. It appeared to be legal.

_____

_____

The passing of the Enabling Act ensured that by the end of March 1933 Germany was well on the way to being a one-party Nazi state.

! Developing an argument

Below are a sample exam-style question, a list of key points to be made in the essay and a paragraph from the essay. Read the question, the plan and the sample paragraph. Rewrite the paragraph in order to develop an argument. Your paragraph should explain why the factor discussed in the paragraph is linked to the question.

To what extent was the Nazi take-over of power in 1933–34 a 'legal revolution'?

Key points

- The appearance of legality
- 'Bringing into line'
- Violence and terror
- The German Labour Front

Sample paragraph

The Nazis moved quickly to bring into line all those parts of the political system that were anti-Nazi. In May 1933 trade unions were abolished. Workers' interests would now be protected by the Nazi-controlled Labour Front. At the same time, the Nazis occupied the offices of the SPD and the Communists, confiscating their funds and closing down their newspapers. In June–July 1933 other parties, like the Centre and Nationalist parties, dissolved themselves and Germany became officially a one-party – Nazi – state. Meanwhile Hitler reorganised the state parliaments so that each now had a Nazi majority. By 1934 all state parliaments were abolished. Different areas were placed under the control of *Gauleiter*.

The impact of the Night of the Long Knives

The situation in 1934

Despite the events of 1933, Hitler was still not totally in control.

- Hindenburg remained as President.
- The army remained outside Nazi control. Troops took an oath of loyalty to the President.
- The 2-million-strong SA was a potential threat. While it had played a crucial role in helping Hitler win power, its violent methods proved something of an embarrassment after 1933. Moreover, many SA men, disappointed at the pace of change and by the fact they did not benefit much from Nazi success, were critical of Hitler.

The SA threat

SA leader Ernst Röhm did not hide his criticism of Nazi actions in 1933–34. Röhm wanted to merge the SA and the army, with both under his control. This alarmed both Hitler and army leaders. Hitler did his best to appease Röhm – without success.

The Night of the Long Knives

Fearing that Röhm was planning a *putsch*, Hitler struck first. On the night of 30 June/1 July 1934 – the Night of the Long Knives – Hitler used detachments of the SS to purge the leaders of the SA and settle scores with other enemies. Some 200 people were killed, including Röhm. Hindenburg and the army leadership supported Hitler's action. At one stroke he had wiped out one threat to his power – the SA – and gained the support of the other – the army.

The death of Hindenburg

When Hindenburg died in August 1934, Hitler combined the offices of Chancellor and President. Henceforward, he was known as the Führer (leader). Civil servants and members of the armed forces now took a personal oath of loyalty to him.

The end of freedom

Under the Third Reich, Germans lost the right to freedom of speech and freedom of assembly. The police could arrest and hold people in custody for any reason or none at all.

The use of terror

In March 1933 Heinrich Himmler established the first concentration camp, for political opponents, at Dachau. By the summer of 1933 almost 30,000 people had been taken into 'protective custody' without trial or the right of appeal. Dachau became the model camp, imposing a system intended to break the spirits of the inmates. The camp guards had total power. Corporal punishment was routinely administered and the barely-fed prisoners were expected to do hard physical labour.

Nazi justice and the courts

All judges were appointed by the Nazi Minister of Justice. Any opposition to National Socialism was deemed to be criminal. A series of harsh laws were introduced against those Germans who opposed or conspired against the Third Reich.

In 1934 Hitler ordered the creation of the People's Court (*Volksgerichtshof*). This made sure that opponents of the Nazis charged with treason were found guilty, even if there was little or no evidence.

The imposition of conformity

The regime kept an eye on people via party officials and some 400,000 block wardens – people who were responsible for local-level political supervision of their neighbourhood. Wardens were expected to spread Nazi propaganda but also monitor their neighbours for signs of deviancy.

The situation by 1935

Thus by 1935 Hitler seemed in total control of Germany.

- The Nazis' political opponents had been crushed.
- While some army leaders remained suspicious of Hitler, after 1934 there was general agreement between the military and the Nazis on rearmament and removing the restrictions of the Treaty of Versailles. Most army leaders also approved of the way Hitler had defeated the Communists and provided Germany with strong government.

Write the question   **a**

The following source relates to the Night of the Long Knives. Having read the source, write an exam-style question using the source. Remember the question must focus on two enquiries.

Assess the value of the source for revealing _____ and _____.

Explain your answer, using the source, the information given about its origin and your own knowledge about the historical context.

SOURCE 1

From Hitler's speech to the Reichstag on 13 July 1934.

At 1:00 in the morning I received two extremely urgent alarm bulletins from Berlin and Munich. Namely first of all, that an alert had been issued in Berlin for 4:00 in the afternoon, that the order had already been given for the requisition of trucks to transport what were actually the raiding formations and that this was already being carried out, and that the action was to begin promptly at the stroke of 5:00 as a surprise attack with the occupation of the government building. This was the reason why Gruppenführer Ernst had not traveled to Wiessee but remained in Berlin in order to conduct the action in person. Second of all, an alert had already been given to the SA in Munich for 9:00 in the evening.

The SA formations would not be allowed to return home but were assigned to the alert barracks. That is mutiny! I am the commander of the SA and no one else! Under these circumstances, there was only one decision left for me to make.

If there was any chance to avert the disaster, lightning action was called for.

Only ruthless and bloody intervention might perhaps still have been capable of stifling the spread of the revolt. And then there could be no question of the fact that it would be better to destroy a hundred mutineers, plotters and conspirators (Meuterer, Verschwörer und Konspiratoren) than to allow ten thousand innocent SA men on the one hand and ten thousand equally innocent persons on the other to bleed to death. For if the plans of that criminal Ernst were set in motion in Berlin, the consequences would be unimaginable! How well the manipulations with my name had worked was evidenced in the distressing fact that these mutineers had, for instance, succeeded in securing four armored vehicles for their action from unsuspecting police officers in Berlin by citing my name, and that furthermore, even before then, the conspirators Heines and Hayn had made police officers in Saxony and Silesia uncertain by demanding that they decide between the SA and Hitler's enemies in the coming confrontation.

It finally became clear to me that only one man could and must stand up to the Chief of Staff. He had broken his vow of loyalty to me, and I alone had to call him to account for that! At 1:00 in the morning, I received the last alarm dispatches, and at 2:00 a.m. I flew to Munich. In the meantime, I had already instructed Minister-President Göring that, in the event of a purge action, he was immediately to take corresponding measures in Berlin and Prussia.

Hitler's role as Führer

Hitler's leadership

The spirit of the Third Reich was embodied in Hitler's remark that there could be only one will in Germany, his own, and that all others had to be subservient to it.

Hitler's power

Hitler saw politics essentially as the actions of great men and the solving of problems as a matter of will power. Decision-making in the Third Reich was therefore inspired by Hitler's personal whim rather than by administrative procedures.

Hitler's leadership style

While Hitler was the only source of real authority, he rarely involved himself in the day-to-day discussions which led to the formulation of policy. Cabinet meetings became less frequent and he did not see some ministers for months at a time. His preference for his home in Bavaria instead of Berlin and his aversion to systematic work meant that decision-making was often a chaotic process.

Authoritarian anarchy?

Nazi propaganda depicted the Third Reich as a well-run regime. However, most historians now think that Hitler's Germany was inefficiently governed.

The relationship of state and party

After 1933 Nazi Germany had two bureaucratic groups:
- existing state ministries
- expanding Nazi Party organisations.

The two functioned uneasily alongside each other, competing to implement policies which Hitler often did little more than outline. The lines of power and authority between state and party blurred amidst the struggle for influence. The Nazi Party itself was by no means a unified whole. It consisted of a mass of organisations like the SS and the Hitler Youth which were keen to uphold their own interests.

Hitler's tendency to create new agencies, with the job of speeding up particular projects, added to the confusion. Powerful figures, like Goering and Himmler, built up their own empires (sometimes involving both state and party organisations), often ignoring everyone except Hitler. Accordingly, there was a proliferation of bureaucracies and agencies and no precise relationship between them.

The structuralist view

The historians Broszat and Mommsen have claimed that the anarchic system controlled Hitler, rather than he the system. In consequence, they believe that historians should focus upon the structure of the Nazi state rather than upon Hitler himself. In this 'structuralist' or 'functionalist' view, many of the Nazi regime's measures, rather than being the result of long-term planning or even deliberate intent, were simply knee-jerk responses to the pressure of circumstance. Mommsen suggests that Hitler was a 'weak dictator', who took few decisions and had difficulty getting these implemented.

Was Hitler a weak dictator?

The structuralists have probably exaggerated the 'authoritarian anarchy' of the Third Reich.
- In reality, there was not always confrontation between party and state bureaucrats.
- The men who staffed both the party and state machinery conducted their business with reasonable efficiency.
- The special agencies often got things done quickly.
- The idea of 'authoritarian anarchy' does not fit the remarkable success of the Third Reich up to 1941.

To view Hitler as a 'weak dictator' is to misconstrue the situation. He was ultimately in control. He did not – could not – concern himself with everything. However, in those areas he considered vital, he showed real firmness of purpose: he made the strategic decisions; subordinates hammered out the details.

! Complete the paragraph   **a**

Below are a sample exam-style question and a paragraph written in answer to this question. The paragraph contains a point and a concluding explanatory link back to the question, but lacks examples. Complete the paragraph, adding examples in the space provided.

> To what extent do you agree with the view that Hitler was a weak dictator?

Immediately after the end of the Second World War, the image of the Nazi state was one that was hierarchically organised, with all power concentrated in Hitler's hands.

_____

_____

Thus, in reality, because of the nature of the Nazi state and his own character, Hitler was rather a weak dictator.

Support or challenge?

Below is a sample A-level exam-style question which asks how far you agree with a specific statement. Below this is a series of general statements which are relevant to the question. Using your own knowledge and the information on the opposite page, decide whether these statements support or challenge the statement in the question and tick the appropriate box.

> 'The Nazi state was too chaotic to allow Hitler to be a strong leader.' How far do you agree with this statement?

STATEMENT	SUPPORT	CHALLENGE
Hitler was ultimately in control in Nazi Germany.		
Decision-making processes in the Third Reich were often inefficient.		
The institutions of the state and the Nazi Party often overlapped.		
Gauleiter were only accountable to Hitler.		
Hitler often set up special agencies to get things done quickly.		
Hitler spent many weeks away from Berlin.		
A direct order from Hitler was carried out with immediate effect.		
Men like Himmler and Goering built up their own empires within the Third Reich.		

A 'totalitarian regime'?

Nazi propaganda depicted Hitler as an all-powerful leader. However, since the 1960s structuralist historians have claimed that organisation and decision-making processes in the Third Reich were so chaotic that Hitler was, in reality, a weak dictator. This debate over the extent of Hitler's power is crucial to another area of controversy: how **totalitarian** was the Nazi state?

Totalitarian?

In many respects Nazi Germany does seem to have been a totalitarian regime.

- It was a dictatorship. The state was organised to carry out Hitler's will, which was the basis for law after the Enabling Act.
- It used terror to silence its opponents.
- It tried to brainwash the people by its use of propaganda.
- It controlled many aspects of life in Germany.
- While Hitler did not always make direct decisions, Nazi policy was developed which reflected his wishes. The leaders of the various ministries tried to anticipate what Hitler would want and formulated policy on this basis. Those who could best implement Hitler's will were most likely to win favour and power. Through the mechanism of 'working towards the Führer', Hitler's vision provided the overall inspiration for policy.
- Hitler regularly held **plebiscites** (in which his policies received overwhelming support), thus giving the appearance that his regime was legitimate and popular.

Intentionalist historians believe that Hitler was a strong dictator. In those areas he considered vital, especially the Jewish 'problem' and foreign policy, he took the strategic decisions. Convinced that he was chosen by providence to lead the Germans in their struggle for greatness, he did not lack firmness of purpose.

Not totally totalitarian?

In many respects, Germany was not a stereotypical totalitarian society.

- Hitler was often out of Berlin and gave few direct orders.
- In Nazi Germany state and party structures were often duplicated and overlapping, creating inefficiency.
- The Nazis did not have total control of the economy. Much was left to big business.
- Hitler, aware of the strength of Christianity, generally co-operated with the Protestant and Catholic Churches.
- Aware of likely opposition from the Catholic Church, in particular, Hitler steered clear of euthanasia policies until 1939.
- The Third Reich did not use terror to the same extent as the **USSR**. Relatively few Germans died as a result of Nazi policies pre-1939.
- The Nazi Party was keen to adopt policies which it knew (from opinion poll testing) were popular with most Germans. In other words, the Nazis followed public opinion as much as vice versa.
- Most Germans did not feel as though they lived under a repressive regime; they often supported Nazi actions and believed in Nazi ideas.
- Hitler was wary of upsetting international opinion, especially American opinion, which might damage Germany's economic recovery.
- Unlike most totalitarian regimes, the Third Reich was open to those wanting to visit it and Germans could also travel freely abroad.

Structuralist historians insist that when decision-making in Nazi Germany is analysed, it seems that Hitler rarely initiated action. If Hitler was a weak dictator, it is hard to claim that the Third Reich was an effective totalitarian dictatorship. This is particularly true if the structure of the state was so chaotic that no one, including Hitler, could ever have full command of it.

RAG – rate the timeline

Below are a sample exam-style question and a timeline of events. Read the question, study the timeline and, using three coloured pens, put a Red, Amber or Green star next to the events to show:

Red: events and policies that have no relevance to the question

Amber: events and policies that have some significance to the question

Green: events and policies that are directly relevant to the question

1 To what extent was the Third Reich a totalitarian state?

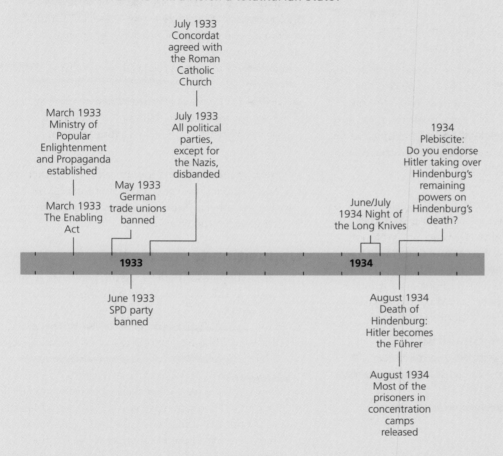

Now repeat the activity with the following questions:

2 'Hitler was a weak dictator and the Nazi state was far less totalitarian than it seemed.' How far do you agree with this statement?

3 To what extent did Hitler's power rest on consensual dictatorship?

Recommended reading

Below is a list of suggested further reading on this section.

- *Hitler: 1889–1936 Hubris*, pages 431–591, Ian Kershaw (1998)
- *The Coming of the Third Reich*, pages 310–461, Richard J. Evans (2003)
- *The Third Reich, A New History*, pages 149–215, Michael Burleigh (2000)

The nature of the new Nazi state

Nazi control

Nazi control was by no means simply dependent on terror.

Nazi propaganda

In 1933 Dr Joseph Goebbels became Minister of Popular Enlightenment and Propaganda.

- Goebbels' ministry was soon responsible for the control of books, the press, the radio and films.
- Goebbels came to control the whole of Germany's art and culture. Painting, sculpture and architecture were all brought under government control.

Goebbels declared that no German should feel him or her self to be a private citizen. The regime constantly urged people to work for the public good and to take part in Nazi activities. Efforts were made to create new kinds of social ritual. The 'Heil Hitler' greeting and the Nazi salute, for example, were intended to strengthen identification with the regime.

Control of youth

The mobilisation of youth was a major goal of the Third Reich. Boys and girls were encouraged to join movements whose aim was to ensure that young Germans were loyal to fatherland and Führer. The Hitler Youth (for boys) placed a strong emphasis on military training. The League of German Maidens emphasised fitness and preparation for motherhood.

Education was also used to indoctrinate.

- Ideologically unreliable teachers were dismissed.
- Subjects like history were used as a vehicle for Nazi ideas.
- Great emphasis was given to physical fitness.

Popular support

Nazi rule did not rest exclusively on intimidation and propaganda. Evidence from Nazi agencies set up to track public opinion suggests that many aspects of Hitler's policies were popular.

- Many Germans supported the idea of a national community (see page 46).
- Most supported Hitler's restoration of national pride.
- Many believed the Nazis had improved the economic situation.

- Many had almost a religious faith in Hitler. He was seen as a great leader, a 'man of the people', working tirelessly on Germany's behalf. Those who were critical of some aspects of policy rarely blamed Hitler. The view was that he would change things 'if only he knew'.

The Churches

Hitler preferred co-operation to conflict with the Churches. Given that he seemed to be upholding traditional values and was strongly anti-Communist, the Protestant and Catholic Churches were prepared to co-operate with him.

- In 1933 Protestants agreed to unite to form a 'Reich Church', electing a Nazi as their 'Reich Bishop'.
- In 1933 Hitler made a Concordat with the Pope. In return for the Catholic Church staying out of German politics, Hitler guaranteed religious freedom for Catholics.

In general, Church leaders sought to avoid conflict with the Nazi regime. Few spoke out about the regime's anti-Jewish policies. Most Christians accepted, many wholeheartedly, the Nazi regime.

Opposition to the Nazis

However, support for Hitler's regime was never total.

- Many workers were far from enthusiastic Nazi supporters.
- While most Germans collaborated with the regime, minor acts of non-conformity, such as refusing to give the Hitler salute, listening to jazz or making anti-Hitler jokes, were relatively common.
- Many Germans were dissatisfied with their economic lot.
- A group of Protestant pastors, led by Martin Niemöller and Dietrich Bonhoeffer, set up the Confessional Church in opposition to attempts to Nazify the Protestant Church.

However, discontent and non-conformity did not translate into a fervent desire to overthrow the Nazi state. Open opposition was difficult because most independent organisations were dissolved and Nazi opponents were arrested. Underground networks of resistance, formed by the Communists and SPD, posed no threat to the regime.

Spectrum of importance

Below are a sample exam-style question and a list of general points which could be used to answer the question. Use your own knowledge and the information in this section to reach a judgement about the importance of these general points to the question posed. Write numbers on the spectrum below to indicate their relative importance. Having done this, write a brief justification of your placement, explaining why some of these factors are more important than others. The resulting diagram could form the basis of an essay plan.

'Nazi popularity in Germany between 1933 and 1935 was largely dependent on propaganda.' How far do you agree with this statement?

1 The difficulty of opposition

2 Nazi terror

3 Joseph Goebbels' propaganda methods

4 Indoctrination of youth

5 Nazi economic success, 1933–35

6 Most Germans agreed with Nazi policies

7 Were Hitler and the Nazis really popular?

Less important   Very important

Develop the detail a

Below are a sample exam-style question and a paragraph written in answer to this question. The paragraph contains a limited amount of detail. Annotate the paragraph to add additional detail to the answer.

To what extent was Nazi rule genuinely popular in Germany between 1933 and 1935?

Nazi propaganda did much to persuade Germans that Nazi rule was a 'good thing'. Germans in the Third Reich were given just one view of the situation: the Nazi view. Joseph Goebbels was crucial to this whole process. Nazi indoctrination of youth was another feature of the way the Nazi regime tried to ensure that Germans, particularly the next generation of Germans, would support Nazi ideology. Nazi propaganda and indoctrination undoubtedly helped convince many Germans that Hitler was some kind of 'superman'.

Attempts to create a *Volksgemeinschaft*

Nazi society

The Nazis claimed to be creating a new and better kind of society, a 'people's community' (*Volksgemeinschaft*), in which the class divisions that had previously rent Germany asunder would cease.

Improved standards of living

Economic recovery ensured that, on balance, the Nazis were able to keep their promise of 'a better deal' for Germans.

- Wages and working conditions improved steadily after 1933.
- The Nazis provided better old age pensions and national health insurance.

Women's role

The role of women in Nazi Germany was central to the aim to build a national community based on common blood and values.

- The Nazis believed women should be confined to their 'natural' roles as wives and mothers.
- Given that the Nazis were keen to increase Germany's population, women were encouraged to leave work, to marry and to breed. Abortion was prohibited, access to contraception restricted and financial incentives given to encourage people to have children. Mothers who had large families were awarded the Mothers' Cross.
- Nazi birth-encouraging policies were successful: in 1936 there were over 30 per cent more births than in 1933.

Social mobility

Hitler aimed to promote social mobility and break down class differences. Some progress was made on this front. Many Germans do seem to have felt an increased sense of comradeship, even if class identities were not eradicated.

Racial policy, 1933–35

While the Nazis were keen to encourage 'good blood', racial aliens and the mentally and physically handicapped were to be 'eliminated'.

New laws

- A 1933 law permitted the compulsory sterilisation of anyone suffering from a hereditary disease and/or deemed to be mentally or physically unfit. Doctors and directors of hospitals, homes and prisons submitted nearly 400,000 names during 1934–35. Over 80 per cent of the cases (examined by 220 new health courts) resulted in sterilisation.
- A 1935 law prohibited a marriage if either party suffered from a mental derangement or had a hereditary disease.

Hitler was keen to go further and introduce a euthanasia programme. But he desisted, aware that this was likely to arouse opposition, especially from the Catholic Church.

Anti-Semitism

In 1933 there were 500,000 Jews in Germany, less than one per cent of the population. Anti-Semitism was an article of faith for Hitler and for many Nazis. While Hitler had not prepared a step-by-step anti-Jewish programme, he certainly had in mind the major lines of future action, including the exclusion of Jews from public office, a ban on Jewish-German marriages and efforts to force Jews to emigrate.

The situation, 1933–35

- In March 1933 Nazi mobs beat up Jews and destroyed Jewish property.
- A flood of laws excluded Jews from specific jobs.
- Anti-Semitic measures were taken by local authorities and by professional organisations.

The Nuremberg Laws

In September 1935 Hitler introduced two new laws at the Nuremberg rally.

- Marriage and sexual relations between Jews and Germans were prohibited.
- Jews lost their German citizenship.

The question of defining just who was Jewish remained a major problem. In November 1935 party and ministry experts agreed that a 'full Jew' was someone who had three Jewish grandparents and was married to a Jew.

Thus by 1935 the Nazis had made life difficult for Jews. Nevertheless, few anticipated the worse measures that were still to come. Only 120,000 Jews had left Germany by 1937.

Spot the inference

High-level answers avoid excessive summarising or paraphrasing a source. Instead they make inferences from the sources as well as analysing their value in terms of their context. Below are a source and a question.

Assess the value of Source 1 German attitudes to women's rights and Hitler's views of *Volksgemeinschaft*. Explain your answer using the source, the information given about its origin and your own knowledge about the historical content.

Below are a series of statements. Read the source and decide which of the statements:

- infer from the source (I)
- paraphrase the source (P)
- summarise the source (S)
- cannot be justified from the source (X).

1 Hitler did not like Jewish intellectuals.
2 Hitler believed that large numbers of German women supported Nazi policy with regard to women's new role.
3 Hitler believed that women were inferior to men.
4 Hitler believed that women's place was essentially in the home.

SOURCE 1

An extract from a speech by Adolf Hitler to the National Socialist Women's League on 8 September 1934. Hitler's views on women's role in society were well known. This speech, which was well publicised at the time, elaborated the official Nazi attitude to women.

The slogan 'Emancipation of women' was invented by Jewish intellectuals and its content was formed by the same spirit. In the really good times of German life the German woman had no need to emancipate herself. She possessed exactly what nature had necessarily given her to administer and preserve; just as the man in his good times had no need to fear that he would be ousted from his position in relation to the woman …

If the man's world is said to be the State, his struggle, his readiness to devote his powers to the service of the community, then it may perhaps be said that the woman's is a smaller world. For her world is her husband, her family, her children, and her home. But what would become of the greater world if there were no one to tend and care for the smaller one? How could the greater world survive if there were no one to make the cares of the smaller world the content of their lives? No, the greater world is built on the foundations of this smaller world. This great world cannot survive if the smaller world is not stable … The two worlds are not antagonistic. They complement each other. They belong together just as man and woman belong together …

It is not true, as Jewish intellectuals assert, that respect depends on the overlapping of the spheres of activity of the sexes; this respect demands that neither sex should try to do that which belongs to the sphere of the other. It lies in the last resort in the fact that each knows that the other is doing everything necessary to maintain the whole community …

So our women's movement is for us not something which inscribes on its banner as its programme the fight against men, but something which has as its programme the common fight together with men. For the new National Socialist national community acquires a firm basis precisely because we have gained the trust of millions of women as fanatical fellow-combatants …

Whereas previously the programmes of the liberal, intellectualist women's movements contained many points, the programme of our National Socialist Women's movement has in reality but one single point, and that point is the child, that tiny creature which must be born and grow strong and which alone gives meaning to the whole life-struggle.

Exam focus

Below are a sample source, question and answer to the question. Read the source. Then read the answer and the comments around it.

Assess the value of Source 1 for revealing information about the passing of the Enabling Law and for revealing SPD attitudes to Hitler and the Nazis in 1933. Explain your answer using the source, the information given about its origin and your own knowledge about the historical context.

SOURCE 1

A Bavarian SPD deputy, Wilhelm Hoegner, describes the passing of the Enabling Act (23 March 1933). His account was published in 1963, 30 years after the event. Hoegner, unlike many of the SPD deputies in the *Reichstag* on 23 March 1933, survived the Third Reich. A member of the *Reichstag* from 1930–33, he had actively opposed the Nazis in Munich in the 1920s. After 1933 he fled first to Austria and then to Switzerland. After 1945, he became Bavarian Prime Minister (1945–47 and 1954–57).

The wide square in front of the Kroll Opera House was crowded with dark masses of people. We were received with wild choruses: 'We want the Enabling Act!' Youths with swastikas on their chests eyed us insolently, blocked our way, in fact made us run the gauntlet, calling us names like 'Centre pig', 'Marxist sow'. The Kroll Opera House was crawling with armed SA and SS men. In the cloakroom we learned that Severing [an SPD leader] had been arrested on entering the building. The assembly hall was decorated with swastikas and similar ornaments ... When we Social Democrats had taken our seats on the extreme left, SA and SS men lined up at the exits and along the walls behind us in a semicircle. Their expressions boded no good.

Hitler read out his government declaration in a surprisingly calm voice. Only in a few places did he raise it to a fanatical frenzy: when he demanded the public execution of van der Lubbe and when, at the end of his speech, he uttered dark threats of what would happen if the *Reichstag* did not vote the Enabling Act he was demanding. I had not seen him for a long time. He did not resemble the ideal of the Germanic hero in any way. Instead of fair hair, a black strand of hair hung down over his sallow face. His voice gushed out of his throat in dark gurgling sounds. I have never understood how this speaker could carry away thousands of people with enthusiasm.

After the government declaration, there was an interval. The former Reich Chancellor, Dr Wirth, came over and said bitterly that in his group the only question had been whether they should also give Hitler the rope to hang them with. The majority of the Centre Party was willing to obey Monseigneur Dr Kaas and let Hitler have his Enabling Act. If they refused, they feared the outbreak of the Nazi revolution and bloody anarchy. Only a few, among them Dr Bruning, were against any concessions to Hitler.

Otto Wels read out a reply to the government declaration. It was a masterpiece in form and content, a farewell to the fading epoch of human rights and humanity. In concluding, Otto Wels, with his voice half choking, gave our good wishes to the persecuted and oppressed in Germany who, though innocent, were already filling the prisons and concentration camps simply on account of their political creed.

The source was published in 1963 (it may have been written much earlier). It provides an account by Wilhelm Hoegner, a Bavarian SPD member of the *Reichstag*, of events in the *Reichstag* on 23 March 1933 as the Nazi Party tried to pass the Enabling Law. Hoegner's account of the situation both inside and outside the *Reichstag* on 23 March can, no doubt, be verified by scores of other accounts by men and women who were there at the same time as Hoegner. It may be that these other accounts, however, will not be as graphic as his.

> A safe and sensible introduction which provides some context to the source.

The *Reichstag* deputies met in the Kroll Opera House because the *Reichstag* building in Berlin was out of action. On 27 February 1933, a Dutch Communist, van der Lubbe (a man actually mentioned in the source), on his own admission, had set fire to the building. The Nazis had used the *Reichstag* Fire to their advantage electorally, winning 44 per cent of the vote in the elections held on 5 March. Their Nationalist Party allies had won 8 per cent of the vote, giving the Nazi–Nationalist coalition a bare majority in the *Reichstag*. Hitler now sought to change the Weimar constitution by passing the Enabling Law which, by allowing the government to pass budgets and promulgate laws, including the alteration of the constitution for four years without parliamentary approval, would effectively give Hitler dictatorial powers. Given that this was a change to the Weimar constitution, Hitler needed a two-thirds majority to pass the Enabling Law. The Nazi Party adopted a number of measures to get the votes it needed. One was to arrest scores of elected Communist and radical SPD deputies, thus preventing them from voting. Another was to reach agreement with the Catholic Centre Party by promising that the new government would not attack the Catholic Church. A final method was intimidation.

> This paragraph is almost all context. The candidate uses own knowledge to provide good detail of the situation on 23 March 1933. The candidate does well to stress the link between the *Reichstag* Fire and both the Nazi election success and the fact that the *Reichstag* was meeting in the Kroll Opera House.

The source describes Nazi methods of intimidation both outside and inside the Opera House. Hoegner, a member of the SPD, the main opposition party to the Nazis, recounts how the Kroll Opera House was surrounded with armed SA and SS men and how, to enter the building, he had to 'run the gauntlet' of a crowd of Nazis shouting abuse and threatening violence. Once inside the building, Hoegner describes how SS and SA men were lined up at the exits and along the walls behind the deputies. The intimidation thus continued.

> This paragraph is generally sound paraphrasing of the source.

Hoegner goes on to describe Hitler's reading of the government declaration. According to Hoegner he spoke calmly – Hoegner does not say for how long – but not, in Hoegner's view, impressively. Hoegner then describes how former Chancellor Dr Wirth came across to the SPD benches to explain why the Centre Party was voting for the measure. Most of its members feared 'revolution and bloody anarchy' if they refused. Consequently, the SPD members would be virtually alone in voting against the Enabling Law. Hoegner praises Otto Wels' brave response to the government's declaration – a speech in which he was critical of the Enabling Law and the fact that the Nazis were already imprisoning their political opponents.

> More paraphrasing which, it should be said, shows a good understanding of the political situation in March 1933.

The SPD's opposition was to no avail. The Enabling Law passed by 444 votes to 94. Its passing gave the destruction of parliamentary democracy an appearance of legality. This was important for the prestige of the Nazi regime both abroad and in Germany. But the truth was that with the Enabling Law's passing, the *Reichstag* had become merely a sounding board for Hitler's major speeches. From now onwards, the legislation of the Third Reich took the form of government laws and Führer edicts.

> Yet more context – but this does probably need to be said. Good knowledge again displayed.

Clearly, Hoegner's account of the situation is useful. He was an eyewitness to an important event. It should be said that it is just one account. Scores of people – other deputies, spectators and newspaper reporters (German and foreign) – described the events of 23 March 1933. Some, like Hoegner, were appalled by what had occurred. Nazi sympathisers obviously saw things differently.

A short paragraph which makes one or two pertinent but not particularly incisive points about the source's value.

The source's limitations as a description of the events of the day are self-evident. Hoegner does not provide much of a time-frame of the events and there are huge gaps in his account. He does not tell us, for example, exactly how long Hitler spoke or tell us what he said. He says nothing about the Nazi deputies' response to Hitler's speech. (Did they clap and cheer?) Nor does he say very much about Wels' response. How long did he speak? How was his speech greeted by the Nazis? Who else – if anyone – spoke? How did Dr Wirth and Dr Bruning, both former Chancellors and both against making concessions to Hitler, actually vote?

This is much – much – better. The paragraph makes some excellent points about the limitations of the source as an account of proceedings.

Hoegner provides an SPD view of proceedings. Presumably he was a relatively moderate SPD deputy. Had he been a radical, he might already have been arrested, like Severing (whom Hoegner mentions). Hoegner was not impressed by Hitler's speech. (It would have been surprising had he been so.) He takes a cheap swipe at the German Chancellor for not resembling the ideal of the blond-haired Germanic hero. Nor is he impressed by his speaking style. Hoegner focuses on those events which concerned him: Nazi intimidation, the actions of the Centre Party, the courage of SPD leader Otto Wels. Hoegner's account of the atmosphere both outside and inside the temporary *Reichstag* provides an indication of the courage needed by the SPD deputies to oppose the Enabling Law. The account also says something of the sorrow and impotence that most SPD deputies must have felt at what was happening – 'a farewell to the fading epoch of human rights and humanity'. No doubt Nazi supporters would have seen things very differently.

This paragraph looks at the second area – SPD attitudes. It makes some trenchant points. The courage point is particularly well made.

The source has limitations with regard to SPD attitudes to the Nazis. It is, after all, just one man's account. It would be surprising if Hoegner's views encompassed the many shades of SPD opinion. Hoegner, for example, is not particularly critical of the actions of the bulk of Centre Party members who supported the passing of the Enabling Law. Other SPD members probably felt bitter from what amounted to Centre Party betrayal. It should be said that Hoegner's criticisms of Hitler and Nazi Party actions, implicit in the source, hardly come as a surprise. Such criticisms would certainly have resonated strongly with all SPD deputies.

This paragraph is a bit thin but makes one or two valid points (e.g. about SPD attitude to the Centre Party).

One of the problems of the source is that it is unclear precisely when Hoegner was writing. Was the account written almost immediately after the event – but not published until three decades later? Or was it written three decades later, with the benefit of hindsight? Did Hoegner get much of his detail of events from other contemporary sources rather than rely on his memory of those events? It is not easy to remember exact words, never mind feelings, many years after an event. Perhaps this does not matter too much. The fact is that Hoegner was present at a crucial moment in the *Reichstag*'s history. The source, whether near 'primary' or written much later, is a sobering account of the end of democracy in Germany. It provides us with vivid details of the events on 23 March 1933 from an SPD perspective.

This is an excellent conclusion. It makes some incisive points about the overall value of the source.

This essay is an analytical response integrating own knowledge with understanding of the source. It displays excellent knowledge of the source's context. It also has important – and interesting – things to say about the source's value in the two areas of the question. The conclusion is particularly effective. The candidate's answer is generally well structured and is certainly well written. In consequence, it should be awarded a Level 5 mark.

What makes a good answer?

You have now considered two high-level source-based essays. Use these essays to make a bullet-pointed list of the characteristics of a top-level essay. Use this list when planning and writing your own practice exam essays.

4 Establishing and ruling the new Federal Republic, 1949–60

The division of Germany, 1945–49

Following the end of the Second World War in 1945, the Allied powers were determined that Germany should never again become a threat to them. But they had no clear or agreed vision of what the new Germany should look like or how it should be governed.

Germany, 1945–48

Germany surrendered on 8 May 1945. The country lay in ruins. Defeat had been total and overwhelming.

The situation in 1945

After Germany's defeat in 1945, the country was partitioned into four occupation zones under the direction of an Allied Control Council.

- Britain occupied north-western Germany.
- The USA occupied southern Germany.
- France occupied south-western Germany.
- The USSR occupied eastern Germany.

Berlin was also divided into four occupation zones. Each of the Allies ran their zone more or less independently in 1945–46.

The start of the Cold War

By 1946–47 the USA, Britain and France were increasingly at odds with the USSR. Given the establishment of Communist regimes across Eastern Europe, the Western powers were determined to stop the USSR winning control of all of Germany.

The Bizone

In January 1947 Britain and the USA merged their zones, uniting 40 million Germans. The creation of the so-called Bizone (or 'Bizonia') established an economic division of Germany. The political division was accelerated in 1947 by the USA's decision to:

- lead the West in resisting Communist expansion, enshrined in the **Truman Doctrine**
- support the Truman Doctrine with financial assistance – the **Marshall Plan**.

Allied moves towards the creation of the FRG

- In early 1948 the USA, Britain and France, together with Belgium, Luxembourg and Holland, held a series of conferences agreeing to the creation of a federal form of government in Western Germany.
- In mid-1948 the French agreed to merge their zone with the Bizone, thereby creating 'Trizonia'.
- In 1948 the USA and Britain pushed ahead with plans to create a new German Central Bank and to introduce a new German currency – the *Deutschmark*. These moves were bitterly opposed by the USSR.

The Berlin Blockade

The USSR retaliated to German currency reform by blockading all road, rail and barge access to West Berlin. The USA and Britain organised a huge airlift of supplies to West Berlin – a remarkable achievement. In May 1949 the USSR finally ceased the blockade of Berlin.

West and East Germany

The blockade ensured the creation of two separate German states in 1949 – the Federal Republic of Germany (FRG) in the West and the German Democratic Republic (GDR) in the East.

The Federal Republic of Germany (FRG)

A Parliamentary Council, elected by each provincial West German government, was formed in August 1948 to draft a provisional constitution. This Council was chaired by Konrad Adenauer, leader of the Christian Democrats (CDU). The constitution (or Basic Law) was approved by the military governors of the three Western zones and the Federal Republic (West Germany) was founded on 23 May 1949. The city of Bonn became the new capital.

The German Democratic Republic (GDR)

Pre-1949 East German Communists, with Soviet backing, attempted (unsuccessfully) to win over opinion for a unified – Communist – Germany. In October 1949 the GDR was founded. East German authorities delayed taking this step until after the creation of the FRG in order not to be seen as leading the process of division. The GDR almost immediately became a Communist dictatorship, led by Walter Ulbricht, head of the Socialist Unity Party of Germany (SED).

Mind map

Use the information on the opposite page to add detail to the mind map below. This should assist your understanding of the situation in Germany between 1945 and 1949.

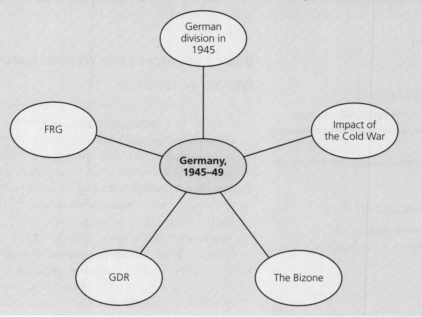

Develop the detail

a

Below are a sample exam-style question and a paragraph written in answer to this question. The paragraph contains a limited amount of detail. Annotate the paragraph to add additional detail to the answer.

To what extent were the Allied powers responsible for the division of Germany in the years 1945–49?

In 1945 Germany was divided into four zones of occupation — British, French, American and Russian. The four powers acted jointly through the Allied Control Council. But generally each of the Allies ran their zones more or less independently. By 1948 the Soviet zone was clearly separate from the Western zones.

The West German constitution

The Basic Law

The Basic Law, which came into force on 23 May 1949, established the FRG as a federal, parliamentary democracy.

The Federal Parliament

This consisted of a lower and upper house:

The lower house (or *Bundestag*)

- Elected every four years through universal suffrage.
- Half its members were directly elected and half elected through party lists.
- Parties needed to win over five per cent of the vote to gain representation.

The upper house (or *Bundesrat*)

- Made up of representatives of each state (or *Land*).
- Had the power to approve and veto legislation.

The President

The President was a largely ceremonial head of state elected by *Bundestag* members and representatives of each state parliament.

The Chancellor

The Chancellor, the head of the government, was elected by the *Bundestag*. The Chancellor could only be removed from office by a 'constructive vote of no confidence' in the *Bundestag*, whereby the removal of one Chancellor depended on the *Bundestag*'s election of a successor.

State parliaments

Substantial powers were given to the state parliaments, as in the 1871 and 1919 constitutions.

The Federal Constitutional Court

This was modelled on the US Supreme Court. It was designed to protect the constitution and had powers to settle disputes between the federal government and state governments. The court was empowered to ban political parties deemed to be undemocratic.

Essential values

The Basic Law set out the essential values of the state.

- There could be no more Enabling Acts or similar constitutional changes that might undermine democratic rule.
- The Basic Law guaranteed freedom of expression, assembly, association and movement.
- It identified the fundamental basic human rights of each German.
- It committed the FRG to work to re-establish a united Germany and guaranteed West German citizenship for all people of German descent.

Checks and balances

The Basic Law was designed to avoid the perceived flaws in the Weimar constitution which had facilitated Hitler's rise to power.

Basic Law versus the Weimar constitution

Weimar constitution

1. Chancellors were weak. They could be forced out of office by a vote of no confidence or by losing the President's confidence, which either required new elections or the appointment of a presidential nominee. This caused great instability in government.
2. The Weimar Republics had strong Presidents with substantial powers. Article 48 allowed the President to rule by decree in times of emergency.
3. Too many political parties led to political fragmentation and short-lived, coalition governments.
4. Extremist parties such as the Nazis and Communists were able to participate in the political process, despite being openly anti-democratic and intent upon destroying the Weimar constitution.
5. The Constitutional Court was weak.

Basic Law

1. Chancellors were strong. They could only be forced out of office by a vote of no confidence which required a new Chancellor to be immediately voted in, thereby avoiding a leadership vacuum.
2. West Germany had weak Presidents.
3. The five per cent rule prevented too many parties being elected to parliament.
4. Anti-democratic parties could be banned.
5. The Constitutional Court had strong powers.

Conclusion: the attempt to reconcile difference and liberty

The Basic Law, which continued as the constitutional framework of the reunited German state after 1990, was an important achievement. Under it, Germans have experienced the greatest political freedom in their history. By limiting the opportunities of extremist parties on the right and left to gain power, the new constitution helped reconcile differences between Germans. It also succeeded in preserving essential liberties.

Quick quizzes at www.hoddereducation.co.uk/myrevisionnotes

! Complete the paragraph   **a**

Below are a sample exam-style question and a paragraph written in answer to this question. The paragraph contains a point and a concluding explanatory link back to the question, but lacks examples. Complete the paragraph, adding examples in the space provided.

To what extent was the Basic Law based on the Weimar constitution?

> The Federal Parliament under the Basic Law was not dissimilar to the Weimar constitution.
>
> _____
>
> _____
>
> Thus, the Basic Law, learning the lessons of the Weimar constitution, tried to ensure that West Germany would have political stability.

↕ Eliminate irrelevance   **a**

Below are a sample exam-style question and a paragraph written in answer to this question. Read the paragraph and identify parts of the paragraph that are not directly relevant to the question. Draw a line through the information that is irrelevant and justify your decisions in the margin.

How far did the founders of the Basic Law learn from the mistakes of those who established the Weimar constitution?

> The Presidents of West Germany had very different powers to those given to the Presidents of the Weimar Republic. Weimar Presidents had been elected by popular vote every seven years. They also held substantial powers, such as those specified in Article 48, which allowed Presidents to rule by decree in times of emergency or government instability. This had been a major problem in Germany, especially in the period 1930–33. In the economic and political crisis following the Wall Street Crash in America in 1929, President Hindenburg had largely ignored the _Reichstag_ and appointed Chancellors he thought were suitable men to run the country. In the end he had appointed Adolf Hitler as Chancellor of Germany on 30 January 1933, even though Hitler did not command a majority in the _Reichstag_. Under the Basic Law, by contrast, Presidents had relatively few powers. Elected by _Bundestag_ members and representatives of each _Land_ parliament, they were largely ceremonial heads of state. They had no power to rule by decree or appoint Chancellors at whim. Lessons had clearly been learned by the Basic Law founders.

The importance of Adenauer and the CDU in shaping the new Federal Republic

West German parties

West Germany's main parties mainly occupied the centre ground.

The Christian Democratic Union (CDU)

The CDU, founded in 1945, was a centre-right party. At its core were Catholics from the former Centre Party. But it also included Protestants, representatives of big business and right-leaning trade unionists. By 1949 most party members:

- believed that a social market economy (see page 98) was the best economic model
- were conservative on social issues
- were staunchly anti-Communist and committed to a policy of integration with the Western powers.

The CDU could count on support from its sister party, the CSU (Christian Social Union), which stood only in Bavaria.

The Free Democratic Party (FDP)

The liberal FDP, founded in 1948, was led by Theodor Heuss. It was determined to protect individual freedoms and supported economic free enterprise.

The Social Democratic Party (SPD)

The SPD presented itself as the party of the working class. Much of its support came from the large cities of northern Germany and the Ruhr industrial region. In 1949, under the leadership of Kurt Schumacher, the party advocated the nationalisation of major industries and centralised economic planning.

The 1949 election

In 1949, the CDU/CSU won 31 per cent of the vote. The SPD, with 29 per cent, was the second-largest party. Adenauer formed a government coalition with the FDP (which polled nearly 12 per cent) and several small parties. He secured a majority of one (his own vote!) – 202 out of 402 votes – for his election as Chancellor. Heuss became West Germany's first President.

Adenauer as Chancellor, 1949–60

In 1949 it seemed that the FRG might return to Weimar instability, with the larger parties dependent on coalitions with smaller parties. Instead, Adenauer remained in power until 1963.

Economic success

Economic recovery was Adenauer's most significant success. This success is most associated with Economics Minister Ludwig Erhard. Erhard, fully committed to market forces, achieved an average of eight per cent growth per annum and ever-rising living standards.

International rehabilitation

- In 1951 Germany joined the European Coal and Steel Community.
- In 1955 West Germany became a member of NATO.
- In 1957 the Bonn Convention saw the return of full German sovereignty.
- In 1957 West Germany signed the Treaty of Rome, becoming a founding member of the European Economic Community.
- Adenauer accepted that West and East Germany would be separate for the foreseeable future.

'Chancellor democracy'

Adenauer's style of leadership has been called 'Chancellor democracy' because of the personal authority he wielded in government. His supporters regarded him as clear-sighted, realistic, tough and uncompromising. His critics saw him as dogmatic, domineering and arrogant.

Political success

In the 1953 election the CDU won 45.2 per cent of the popular vote. (Its coalition partner the FDP won 9.5 per cent.) In 1957, *Der Alte* (The Old Man), as Adenauer was nicknamed, won 50.2 per cent of the vote. This success was largely the result of Adenauer's record of achievement and a general feel-good factor. By the mid-1950s, the CDU had also developed an efficient party organisation which appealed to a wide cross-section of German society.

However, Adenauer's third (and later fourth) governments were characterised by a gradual diminishment in his authority. Several political miscalculations and scandals dominated Adenauer's later years.

ⓘ Write the question ⓐ

The following source relates to the situation in West Germany in 1949. Having read the source, write an exam-style question using the source. Remember the question must focus on two enquiries.

Assess the value of the source for revealing _____ and _____.

Explain your answer, using the source, the information given about its origin and your own knowledge about the historical context.

SOURCE 1

An extract from a speech given by Konrad Adenauer at a reception given by the Allied High Commissioners on 21 September 1949. Adenauer, the leader of the Christian Democratic Union, had just become the first Chancellor of the FRG. While the FRG now had considerable independence, it did not have full sovereignty. The Allied powers still had certain rights within Germany.

Now that the German Federal Assembly has convened and the Federal president been elected, and now that I have been chosen Federal Chancellor and the members of the Federal Cabinet have been appointed, a new chapter of German history of the post-war years begin. The disaster of the Second World War has left in its wake a Germany almost totally destroyed. Our cities were in ruins. Economic life was largely smashed. All vestiges of government had ceased. The very souls of men had suffered injuries that it seemed doubtful whether a recovery would ever be possible … It is fitting and proper to acknowledge gratefully that the German population was saved during these trying years from starvation by Allied help in supplying food … It was this help which made possible the start of reconstruction. Now that the governmental and legislative elements of the German Federal Republic are being built up, a large part of the responsibility and authority to make decisions will pass into German hands. We do not, of course, possess as yet complete freedom, since there are considerable restrictions contained in the occupation statute. We will do our part to bring about an atmosphere in which the Allied powers will see their way clear to apply the occupation statute in a liberal and genuine manner; only in this way will the German people be able to attain full freedom. We hope that the Allied powers will, by making a corresponding use of the revision clause in the occupying statute, hasten the further political development of our country.

It is the unshakable wish of the new Federal Government first and foremost to tackle the great social problems. The Government is convinced that a sound political entity can only develop when each individual is assured a maximum of economic opportunity to earn a livelihood. Not until we succeed in converting the flotsam millions of refugees into settled inhabitants by providing them with housing and adequate opportunities for work will we be able to enjoy inner stability in Germany …

If we want to establish peace in Europe, we can, in the view of the Federal Government, achieve this only by working along entirely new methods. We see opportunities to do so in the efforts for a European federation which has just borne its first fruits at Strasbourg. We do believe, however, that such a federation will only have a vitality if built on close economic cooperation among the nations. The organization created by the Marshall Plan represents a good start in this direction. Germany is fully ready to cooperate responsibly. In this regard … we are certain that the narrow nationalistic conception of the state as it prevailed in the nineteenth and early twentieth centuries may now be said to be overcome.

Changes in the nature of the SPD and its significance for the shaping of the Federal Republic

SPD problems, 1949–52

The SPD was Germany's oldest political party. It faced problems in and after 1949.

SPD leadership and support

- Many of the SPD's former leaders had died during the Third Reich. Kurt Schumacher, SPD leader from 1945, had spent ten years in Dachau concentration camp. Although a charismatic figure, his health was broken and he had lost an arm and a leg.
- Many of the SPD's former political strongholds were now in East Germany whereas the staunchly conservative regions of Bavaria and the Rhineland were in the West.

The Communist threat

In the late 1940s the SPD faced a threat from the Communist Party (KPD). KPD leaders, selected and trained in the USSR, proclaimed that they supported a 'reformist' programme and declared their determination to uphold the rights of private property and free enterprise. This cynical attempt to win over SPD voters was strongly opposed by Schumacher. A bitter enemy of the KPD, Schumacher's opposition helped to ensure that most German workers remained loyal to the SPD.

The 1949 election

In 1949, the SPD adopted a left-wing economic programme, supporting the nationalisation of major industries and centralised economic planning. Schumacher, a German nationalist, rejected Adenauer's Western-orientated policy. Instead, he prioritised German reunification, even if this meant reaching some kind of arrangement with the USSR. The SPD won 29.2 per cent of the vote, not enough to stop Adenauer becoming Chancellor.

The situation, 1949–52

- The West German 'economic miracle' proved to most people that CDU economic policies were more successful than those of the SPD.
- Most West Germans preferred the security of American support to SPD demands for German unity.
- Communist actions in East Germany created an anti-socialist backlash in West Germany, no matter how vociferously Schumacher condemned such actions.

The SPD, 1952–60

Schumacher's death in 1952 led to Erich Hollenhauer becoming SPD leader. Although he was more moderate than Schumacher, he lacked the latter's charisma. He also lacked policies to challenge Adenauer's dominance.

The 1953 and 1957 elections

The SPD won 28.8 per cent of the vote in 1953 and 31.8 per cent in 1957 – not enough to challenge Adenauer.

Willy Brandt

Elections in West Berlin 1958 resulted in **Willy Brandt** becoming SPD mayor. Brandt was a new type of Social Democrat – pro-Western and ready to compromise. His modernising ideas were reflected in the SPD's new programme, adopted at Godesberg in 1959. The SPD now:

- endorsed the free market economy
- fully supported NATO
- announced that it was no longer a party of the working class but an open-ended people's party.

In 1960 the SPD made Brandt their candidate for Chancellor, a youthful alternative to Adenauer who was now in his 80s. Adenauer still won the 1961 election but lost almost 5 per cent of the vote compared with 1957. The SPD, although well beaten, gained 4.4 per cent.

The FDP

The liberal FDP was opposed to the CDU's clericalism and the SPD's socialism. But as the CDU became less clerical and the SPD less socialist, it found it difficult to offer an alternative to the two main parties. Its importance rested largely on the fact that without its support neither the CDU nor the SPD could form a government.

Simple essay style

Below is a sample exam-style question. Use your own knowledge and the information on the opposite page to produce a plan for this question. Choose four general points and provide three pieces of specific information to support each general point. Once you have planned your essay, write the introduction and conclusion for the essay. The introduction should list the points to be discussed in the essay. The conclusion should summarise the key points and justify which point was the most important.

> How accurate would it be to say that the SPD was largely irrelevant in West Germany in the years 1949–60?

Spectrum of significance

Below are a sample exam-style question and a list of general points which could be used to answer the question. Use your own knowledge and the information on the opposite page to reach a judgement about the importance of these general points to the question posed. Write numbers on the spectrum below to indicate their relative importance. Having done this, write a brief justification of your placement, explaining why some of these factors are more important than others. The resulting diagram could form the basis of an essay plan.

> To what extent did the SPD play a significant role in West Germany in the years 1949–60?

1 SPD problems in 1949

2 The leadership of Kurt Schumacher

3 The SPD's anti-Communist stance

4 SPD problems, 1949–52

5 The 1953 and 1957 elections

6 The influence of Willy Brandt

7 The SPD's role as the main opposition party, 1949–60

⟵──────────────────────────────────────⟶

Less important   **Very important**

The process and significance of denazification

The punishment of Nazis

The victorious Allies, while far from united in 1945, did agree that all traces of Nazism had to be destroyed.

War crime trials

Twelve trials of major Nazi war criminals involving over a hundred defendants took place in Nuremberg from 1945 to 1949. The first trial, which began in November 1945, involved the prosecution of 21 Nazi leaders. Eighteen were found guilty, eleven were executed, three received life sentences and four received prison sentences ranging from ten to twenty years.

Overall, in Western-controlled zones more than 5,000 Germans were convicted of crimes against humanity. Nearly 500 were eventually executed.

The impact of the trials

One of the Nuremberg trials' intentions was to make Germans face up to the horror of Nazi atrocities. Although many Germans questioned their legitimacy, the trials did ensure that the Nazi regime's criminality was well documented and publicised. By so clearly establishing the guilt of Nazi leaders, the trials may have allowed Germans to rid themselves of any feeling of collective guilt. They could claim that they were as much victims of the Nazi regime as anyone else.

Denazification

Denazification was a sensitive process.
- Nazi ideology had permeated many aspects of German life.
- Most Germans who had lived through the Third Reich tried to dissociate themselves from the Nazi regime and resented 'prying' investigations into their past conduct.
- Denazification was problematic because of the difficulties of proof, of identifying the guilty and of determining appropriate punishments.

The original plan to disallow important jobs to former Nazis began to unravel almost immediately because of the need to rebuild Germany. It was difficult to find skilled people who had not been tainted in some way by association with Nazism.

Different processes

There were many inconsistencies in denazification application.

The American zone

The Americans initially went about the denazification process zealously. They listed 3.5 million Germans as 'chargeable cases' – a quarter of the total population of their zone. But American zeal diminished as the Cold War developed.

The British and French zones

- The British were prepared to allow ex-Nazis to hold prominent positions.
- The French gave denazification very low priority.

The Soviet zone

The USSR used the denazification programme to get rid of all kinds of opponents, including Communist dissidents, 'bourgeois' democrats and 'capitalists'. Up to 120,000 people were imprisoned in former Nazi concentration camps. Some 40,000 died of ill-treatment. Ex-Nazis who were willing to conform to Communism often remained in public office.

The coming of the Cold War brought a halt to denazification in 1948.

Adenauer's policy

Adenauer felt that many so-called Nazis had simply done their duty as soldiers or civil servants. After 1949, he preferred that the Nazi issue be swept under the carpet. He was thus prepared to employ ex-Nazis in important positions.

The results

- It was impossible to punish all ex-Nazis in the late 1940s. Many serious criminals therefore managed to avoid prosecution.
- Denazification met with considerable opposition from Germans.
- Pro-Nazi sentiment persisted into the post-war period. A 1952 opinion poll suggested that 25 per cent of West Germans still had a 'good opinion' of Hitler.
- The denazification process, while probably inadequate, was sufficient to ensure that West Germany was non-Nazi.

Support or challenge?

Below is a sample exam-style question which asks how far you agree with a specific statement. Below this is a series of general statements which are relevant to the question. Using your own knowledge and the information on the opposite page, decide whether these statements support or challenge the statement in the question and tick the appropriate box.

How successful was denazification in the years 1945–60?

	SUPPORT	CHALLENGE
The main Nazi leaders were tried and executed.		
Germans were made aware of the Nazi regime's crimes.		
Many Germans believed they were victims of the Nazi regime.		
The Allies needed to use the skills of former Nazis in rebuilding Germany.		
The Allies' policy towards denazification was inconsistent.		
Adenauer preferred to sweep the Nazi issue under the carpet.		
Many former Nazis served in Adenauer's government between 1949 and 1960.		

You're the examiner

Below are a sample exam-style question and a paragraph written in answer to the question. Read the paragraph and the mark scheme provided on page 111. Decide which level you would award the paragraph. Write the level below along with a justification for your choice.

How far do you agree that the Allied denazification process in the years 1945–49 was mainly a failure?

> The leading Nazi war criminals were tried at Nuremberg between 1945 and 1949. Some 500 of the main people responsible for horrific crimes against humanity were found guilty and executed. Although many Germans at the time questioned the legitimacy of the trials, they at least made the German people face up to the full horror of Nazi atrocities. At a time when many Germans preferred to forget their involvement with the Nazi regime, the trials served an important purpose: the documentation of Nazi crimes presented at Nuremberg ensured that the criminality of Hitler's regime could not be escaped. The trials made it clear that crimes committed by individuals in support of state ideology remained the responsibility of the individual. This aspect of the denazification process was thus by no means a failure.

Level:

Mark:

Reason for choosing this level and this mark:

_____

_____

'Coming to terms with the past' in the 1950s

The Nazi legacy

In the 1950s many Germans were reluctant to come to terms with their Nazi past.

Government restitution

- In 1952, the FRG agreed to pay the new state of Israel 3.5 billion *Deutschmarks* in compensation for the Holocaust.
- In 1953 a restitution law, which provided compensation for those who had suffered under the Nazi regime, was passed. But only people with a territorial connection to Germany could claim. Of the 42,000 survivors of Buchenwald concentration camp, only 700 were entitled to compensation.

Adenauer's attitude

A meaningful national debate about Nazi crimes was prevented by Adenauer's inclination to sweep the issue under the carpet. The incompleteness of denazification meant that many high-ranking ex-Nazis held prominent roles in political, business and public life in the FRG. Hans Globke, Adenauer's chief of staff (1953–63), for example, had been one of the authors of the 1935 Nuremberg Laws (see page 46). Moreover, Adenauer's government freed many Nazi war criminals.

Denial

In the 1950s the Nazis tended to be portrayed as a small clique of criminals, entirely unrepresentative of German society. While the Nazi regime was castigated, the heroism of German servicemen in the Second World War was glorified and celebrated in memoirs, novels, newspaper articles, films, magazines and comics.

Philosopher Theodor Adorno, in a speech on German television in 1959, criticised Germans for 'wilfully forgetting' their Nazi past. Perhaps the war created a communication gap between wives and husbands, neither volunteering their experiences of home and battle front beyond banal generalisations.

West German commitment to democracy

In 1949 the Western Allies wondered whether the FRG could provide a stable democracy. Many feared that Weimar conditions would re-surface, resulting in the reappearance of authoritarian government and possibly a revival of Nazism.

Political stability

The political fragmentation feared in 1949 did not occur. The safeguards built into the constitution, particularly the five per cent rule, contributed to the FRG's stability. Single-issue parties occasionally won seats but rarely kept them. The All-German Bloc/League of Expellees and Deprived of Rights, for example, gained 27 seats in 1953. But it failed to reach the electoral threshold in 1957 and dwindled away.

Economic success

West Germany's economic success was vital in ensuring support for democracy, contrary to the way in which economic depression had led many Germans to abandon Weimar democracy.

Anti-Communism

Anti-Communism provided an alternative ideological pathway to Nazism, leading West Germans towards accepting democratic values.

The reintegration of ex-Nazis

Arguably the reintegration of former Nazis into key positions in society assisted democracy. Many of Germany's most talented individuals (in all walks of life) had either worked for or conformed to the Nazi state. It would have been much more difficult to build a successful state without making use of their experience.

Adenauer's achievement

In many respects, Adenauer deserves his reputation as the 'founding father' of West German democracy. A committed opponent of both Communism and Nazism, he helped ensure that Bonn democracy did not go the same way as Weimar democracy. Rather than strive for German reunification (an impossibility in the 1950s), he built a stable, prosperous state – a state that would eventually undermine the GDR by acting as a magnet of freedom and prosperity for East Germans.

Complete the paragraph

Below are a sample exam-style question and a paragraph written in answer to this question. The paragraph contains a point and specific examples, but lacks a concluding explanatory link back to the question. Complete the paragraph, adding this link in the space provided.

'West Germany's commitment to democracy in the period 1949–60 is proof that West Germans had abandoned Nazism and all it stood for.' How far do you agree with this statement?

There is no doubt that throughout the period 1949–60 West Germans were committed to democracy. In 1949 the Western Allies wondered whether the FRG could provide a stable democracy. Many feared that Weimar conditions would re-surface, resulting in the reappearance of authoritarian government and possibly a revival of Nazism. Neither the political fragmentation nor the revival occurred. The safeguards built into the constitution, particularly the five per cent rule, contributed to the FRG's stability. So did West Germany's economic success. This was vital in ensuring support for democracy, contrary to the way in which economic depression had led many Germans to abandon Weimar democracy. Nor is there any doubt that Chancellor Adenauer was committed to democracy.

_____

_____

Introducing an argument

Below are a sample exam-style question, a list of key points to be made in the essay, and a simple introduction and conclusion to the essay. Read the question, the plan, and the introduction and conclusion. Rewrite the introduction and conclusion in order to develop an argument.

To what extent did West Germans 'come to terms with their past' in the years 1949–60?

Key points
- The Nazi legacy
- Denazification
- Government restitution
- Adenauer's attitude
- German denial
- West German commitment to democracy

Introduction

The Third Reich had a substantial impact on Germany. The extent to which Germans 'came to terms' with this past is a subject of debate. In the 1950s both the West German government and West Germans tried to sweep the issue under the carpet.

Conclusion

Throughout the 1950s most West Germans saw themselves as victims of the Nazi regime, rather than active supporters and participants. Most West Germans, from Chancellor Adenauer downwards, thought the best way of dealing with the Nazi legacy was to ignore it. They thus did not, in fairness, 'come to terms' with their Nazi past.

Exam focus

Below are an exam-style question and model answer. Read it and the comments around it.

To what extent does Konrad Adenauer deserve his reputation as the 'founding father of West German democracy' in the years 1949–60?

Konrad Adenauer became the first Chancellor of the FRG in 1949 at the age of 73. He remained Chancellor until 1963 when, aged 87, he reluctantly gave up office. A poll of German people conducted in 2003 ranked Adenauer as the 'Best German' ever. He is seen as the man responsible for West Germany's rapid political, economic and moral re-birth. But does he deserve such accolades? It could be that he benefited from, rather than created, the 'economic miracle' of the 1950s. Ultimately, this miracle probably had more to do with the establishment of West German democracy than Adenauer.

> The introduction begins rather blandly. Nevertheless, it does, by the end, focus on the question and provide some indication of where the essay is likely to go.

Adenauer, ex-mayor of Cologne (1917–33), was a Catholic Rhinelander who detested Prussian Protestantism. A prominent Centre Party politician, he had been lucky to escape death in 1944. He became first leader of the Christian Democratic Union Party (CDU) in 1945. The party espoused a Christian approach to politics, conservative on social issues, while advocating a social market model of the economy. It was also strongly anti-Communist and committed to a Western-orientated foreign policy. The CDU won 31 per cent of the vote in August 1949. Refusing to work with the SPD, the second party, which obtained 29.2 per cent of the vote, Adenauer united with the CSU (the CDU's Bavarian sister party), the FDP (Free Democratic Party) and a number of smaller parties. He secured a majority of just one (his own vote!) for his election as Chancellor. It seemed in 1949 that there was a real danger of a return to Weimar instability. But the safeguards built into the Basic Law (particularly the five per cent rule), which Adenauer had helped draw up, ensured that West Germany did not repeat the fatal mistakes of the Weimar constitution.

> While showing detailed knowledge, this paragraph never quite gets to grips with the set question.

Economic recovery was Adenauer's most significant domestic success. The rapid upturn in the economy is usually associated with Ludwig Erhard, Adenauer's Economics Minister (1949–63). Erhard essentially believed in free market forces. But he also accepted that the state should provide assistance to the less fortunate in society. After 1949, Erhard swept away rationing, import controls and bureaucratic regulation. West Germany achieved an astonishing average growth rate through the 1950s of eight per cent per year. Living standards rose 58 per cent between 1953 and 1960, more than double the 25 per cent increase in the UK in the same period.

> This paragraph links back to the introduction. However, it does not really link back to the set question.

Adenauer's government had other achievements, sometimes summarised as the five Rs. The first R was Reconstruction. The 1950 Construction Law provided grants and subsidies for a massive house-building programme, resulting in 4 million new homes by 1957. The second R – Reintegration – ensured that millions of refugees and expellees were dispersed from 'holding camps' and integrated into work and accommodation. As a result of the third R (Restitution), compensation was paid to victims of Nazi crimes. Grants and pensions were also made available to German civilians who had suffered significant losses, particularly to property, as a result of wartime bombing. The fourth R – Restoration – allowed ex-Nazis to be employed as civil servants, leading to the re-employment of over 150,000 Germans who had previously lost their jobs as a result of denazification measures. Adenauer, who had long opposed denazification, claiming it would help foster extreme German nationalism, did his best to sweep the Nazi issue under the carpet. The last R – Relations – concerned the government's relations with trade unions. The 1949 Collective Bargaining Law effectively de-politicised the unions by focusing industrial relations on enhanced productivity rather than wealth redistribution through pay bargaining.

> This paragraph demonstrates a good knowledge of Adenauer's achievements. Unfortunately, it tends to forget the set question.

By the mid-1950s other factors were emerging to ensure Adenauer's continued success. His pro-American, anti-Communist leanings and support for Western integration had been bitterly opposed by the SPD opposition. SPD leader Schumacher labelled Adenauer the 'Chancellor of the Allies', accusing him of putting good relations with the West ahead of Germany's national interest – unification. But most West Germans seem to have regarded American support as of greater importance than calls for an impossible unity with the GDR. Similarly West Germans preferred European co-operation, such as the Council of Europe and the European Coal and Steel Community, promoted by Adenauer, to SPD denunciations that such measures abandoned what little was left of German sovereignty. By 1955 Adenauer obtained membership of NATO, and in 1956 reintroduced a German military force, the *Bundeswehr*. He had also forged a strong alliance with France, Germany's traditional enemy.

> The paragraph stresses Adenauer's success. But it needs to relate the (good) information to the question.

Not surprisingly, Adenauer's perceived record of achievement translated into electoral success. The 1953 election, following in the wake of an unsuccessful anti-Communist uprising in East Germany, increased the CDU's lead over the SPD from 400,000 to 4.5 million votes. In 1957, campaigning under the slogan 'No Experiments', Adenauer won 50.2 per cent of the vote – 18.4 per cent more than the SPD opposition. He was assisted by the USSR's brutal crushing of the 1956 Hungarian uprising and by a generous West German pension scheme introduced in early 1957. *Der Alte* (The Old Man), as Adenauer was affectionately nicknamed, was able to rule without needing the support of coalition allies. Unfortunately, his third and fourth governments were characterised by a gradual decline in both his authority and his popularity, despite an economy that continued to boom. A series of political miscalculations and scandals, and a prolonged fall-out with Erhard, dominated his later years.

> This paragraph, although well-written, follows the trend of the others. It is very much a case of the candidate writing all she or he knows about Adenauer.

Adenauer's style of leadership has been called 'Chancellor democracy' because of the dominating personal authority he wielded in government. His supporters praised him as a tough, uncompromising politician, clear in his assessment of the art of the possible. But his critics, then and now, see his rule as akin to that of Bismarck. They claim that he treated his ministers as mere extensions of his own authority and see him as a dogmatic, arrogant leader, intolerant of contrary opinions.

> A short but reasonably sweet paragraph on Adenauer's style of leadership which was not necessarily very democratic.

There is no doubt that the state of German democracy was far stronger in 1960 than it had appeared in 1949. The political fragmentation which had helped bring about the downfall of the Weimar Republic had not occurred. The safeguards built into the constitution contributed to the FRG's political stability. So did West Germany's economic success. By 1960 it was apparent that the FRG way was far better than the GDR way. Adenauer's rule, based on clear and simple goals, also assisted West Germany. It helped silence criticism from the extreme right and left and also helped to build a stable, democratic, and prosperous state. To this extent, Adenauer deserves his reputation as the founding father of West German democracy.

> The essay is saved by the conclusion which is well-focused on the set question. It raises an issue not raised in the essay – silencing criticism from the right. But, overall, it does pull together much that has been said in the essay.

This is a Level 4 essay. It contains a number of general points that show some understanding of the set question. It is certainly well written and demonstrates a detailed and wide-ranging knowledge of the period. It contains some analysis but unfortunately this is not fully sustained.

Moving from a Level 4 to Level 5

The exam focus essay at the end of Section 2 (pages 34–35) provided a Level 5 essay. The essay here achieves a Level 4. Read both essays, and the comments provided. Make a list of the additional features required to push a Level 4 essay into Level 5.

5 Reunification: recreating a united Germany, 1989–90

The situation in East Germany in 1989

The situation in East Germany (GDR) was to bring about German reunification.

East German problems

Many East Germans had little loyalty to the GDR.
- The GDR was far less wealthy than West Germany.
- The Socialist Unity Party of Germany (SED) had governed the GDR for 40 years without ever being legitimised in a democratic election.
- The SED maintained its position of power through a huge security apparatus. The cornerstone of this system was the Ministry for State Security – the Stasi.
- East Germans were aware that their system was corrupt. Communist leaders enjoyed expensive homes and luxury cars.

The building of the Berlin Wall in 1961 symbolised East Germany's situation. The country had only been able to hold on to its citizens by walling them in.

East German achievements

Some East Germans were proud of their state's achievements:
- The GDR was economically the most successful USSR **satellite state**.
- East Germany achieved huge sporting success thanks to the performance of their (often skilfully doped) athletes, particularly in the Olympic Games.

By the 1980s East Germany had a distinct national identity. Few Germans, East or West, envisaged the creation of a united nation in early 1989.

Problems in the USSR

By the mid-1980s the USSR had serious economic and political problems. In 1985 **Mikhail Gorbachev** became Soviet leader. He was anxious to reform the USSR through his policies of *glasnost* (openness) and *perestroika* (restructuring). In 1986 Gorbachev abandoned the 'Brezhnev Doctrine' which limited the sovereignty of the socialist states in Eastern Europe. It was replaced with the (so-called) 'Sinatra Doctrine' whereby the USSR's satellite states were given a degree of freedom to do things 'their way'.

The situation in Hungary and Poland

- In April 1989 the entire Hungarian **Politburo** was replaced and a number of leading reformers were among the new members.
- In mid-1989 the Polish government officially recognised Solidarity – the main opposition group. An element of democracy was introduced into the political system. This resulted in a triumph for Solidarity.

Erich Honecker and East Germany

East Germany, under SED leader **Erich Honecker**, remained a bastion of old-style Communism. Honecker's regime strongly opposed liberal reform. Any signs of opposition were firmly suppressed.

The opening of borders

The opening of the border between Hungary and Austria in May 1989 allowed East Germans to travel to the West via Hungary. Disaffected East Germans poured into the offices of West Germany's permanent representative in East Berlin, hoping they would be allowed to travel to the FRG. They did the same in FRG embassies in Budapest, Warsaw and Prague. By late August 25,000 East Germans had moved to West Germany. The exodus continued through September.

Trouble in Dresden

On 3 October, the East German government, anxious that the coming celebration of the fortieth anniversary of the state's foundation should not be marred by the spectacle of a mass exodus, closed the frontier with Czechoslovakia. On 4 October the railway station in Dresden was occupied by people hoping to leave East Germany. Police efforts to move the protestors led to injuries on both sides.

Gorbachev's visit to Berlin

By early October, it was clear that resistance to the GDR regime was growing. On 7 October Gorbachev visited Berlin. He urged Honecker to support reform – without success.

! Mind map

Use the information on the opposite page to add detail to the mind map below. This will assist your understanding of East Germany's problems in 1989.

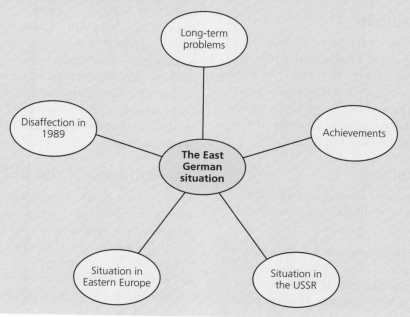

! Introducing an argument

Below are a sample exam-style question, a list of key points to be made in the essay, and a simple introduction and conclusion for the essay. Read the question, the plan, and the introduction and conclusion. Rewrite the introduction and the conclusion in order to develop an argument.

'Problems in the USSR were the main cause of the problems in East Germany in 1989.' How far do you agree with this statement?

Key points
- East German long-term problems
- East German stability
- USSR problems
- The situation elsewhere in Eastern Europe
- The opening of the borders

Introduction

In late 1989 the GDR was in some difficulty. Its problems mainly arose from the situation in the USSR, which had repercussions across Eastern Europe as well as in East Germany.

Conclusion

Although East Germany had plenty of problems, it is unlikely these problems would have come to a head in 1989 had it not been for the situation in the USSR. Soviet problems led directly to problems for the GDR.

Revolution 'from below'

By 1989 East Germany has been described by historian Lothar Kettenacker as a 'downhill train out of control'.

The Civic Revolution

By autumn 1989 a variety of protest movements were developing in East Germany. These included the Civic Movement, New Forum, Democracy Now, Democratic Awakening and the Greens. ('Civic Revolution' is the umbrella term for the protest movement.) Most groups did not support German reunification. Essentially they wanted democratic decision-making.

Growing opposition

By October 1989 opposition was so widespread that the Stasi was unable to stop the increasing number of demonstrations in favour of democratic reform.

Leipzig, a city of 500,000 people, became the centre of opposition.
- On 25 September the first Monday demonstration occurred, involving 10,000 people. The police used relatively little force.
- On 2 October (the following Monday), 20,000 people gathered. Some 20 arrests were made.
- A demonstration of some 1,000 people in East Berlin on 7 October was broken up: over 500 people were arrested.
- On 9 October, some 70,000 protestors defied the Stasi to gather in Leipzig. Honecker wanted to crush the demonstrations. But he was blocked by Egon Krenz, deputy chairman of the council of state, who had the backing of the Soviet ambassador in East Berlin. Krenz's supporters won a major victory over the old guard at Politburo meetings on 10 and 11 October.
- The Monday demonstration in Leipzig on 16 October saw a crowd of 120,000 gather. There were also demonstrations elsewhere.

The end of Honecker

On 18 October Honecker was forced to resign as head of the SED and as head of state. He was replaced by Krenz. In his first public address, Krenz announced that he supported Gorbachev's policy of *perestroika*. Moreover, he lifted restrictions on travel to 'socialist brother-states'; 10,000 people took advantage of this between 1–3 November, travelling to West Germany via Czechoslovakia. After 3 November anyone who had an identity card and enough petrol could drive from East to West Germany.

The collapse of the SED regime

Krenz was too closely associated with the system to win the confidence of civil rights activists. Protest demonstrations continued to spread.
- On 30 October, 300,000 people took part in the Monday rally in Leipzig.
- On 4 November, a massive demonstration (possibly involving one million people) took place in East Berlin. It was shown live on television.

On 8 November all the members of the Politburo resigned. Their replacements included a number of reformers. The SED's Central Committee met on 8 November. Its members were informed that the East German state was virtually bankrupt. Party stalwarts, realising that they had persistently been told a pack of lies, lost faith in the SED.

The fall of the Berlin Wall

On 9 November the Central Committee agreed that the opening of the border to West Germany should take place with effect from 10 November. News of this was quickly relayed on West German television. East Berliners now poured across the border; the border guards took no action. Berlin was once again one city. Berliners celebrated the occasion throughout the night of 9–10 November. On 12 November East Germany began dismantling the Berlin Wall.

Develop the detail

Below are a sample exam-style question and a paragraph written in answer to the question. The paragraph contains a limited amount of detail. Annotate the paragraph to add additional detail to the answer.

To what extent was Germany a 'downhill train out of control' by November 1989?

In late September and early October, there were signs of growing unrest in East German cities. Leipzig, one of the main centres of opposition, had a number of Monday demonstrations, which grew in size each week. By mid-October it was clear that Honecker was in danger of losing control.

Support or challenge?

Below is a sample exam-style question which asks how far you agree with a specific statement. Below this is a series of general statements which are relevant to the question. Using your own knowledge and the information on the opposite page, decide whether these statements support or challenge the statement in the question and tick the appropriate box.

How accurate is to say that the events in East Germany in October and November 1989 were a 'revolution from below'?

	SUPPORT	CHALLENGE
There were many protest movements in East Germany by October 1989.		
There were increasing protests, especially in Leipzig.		
Honecker lost the backing of the USSR.		
Egon Krenz, deputy chairman of the council of state, broke with Honecker.		
In October the SED forced Honecker to resign.		
By November the SED was divided.		
By November the SED had lost control of East Berlin.		
On 9–10 November East Berliners poured into West Berlin.		

West Germany's response to the East German revolt

REVISED

The role of Chancellor Kohl

Helmut Kohl had been in power in West Germany since 1983. By 1989 he was not particularly popular. His government had been hit by political and financial scandal and there was growing support for left- and right-wing political parties. On 10 November, at a mass rally in West Berlin, Kohl urged caution and careful consideration of the significance of the dramatic events in East Germany. His speech was frequently interrupted by whistles and hoots of derision. Pressures in East and West Germany forced Kohl to take action.

The situation in East Germany

By late 1989 the GDR seemed to be in a state of meltdown. In political terms, the East German government had lost most of its authority. A public opinion poll in late November showed that 70 per cent of East Germany's population favoured unification with the West. The dire economic state of the GDR was in some respects more serious. In November 1989, 133,000 East Germans moved to the West. The GDR economy was on the point of collapse.

The situation in West Germany

- The right-wing Republican Party within West Germany, already making political headlines for its anti-immigration agenda, put reunification at the top of its campaign priorities.
- The Bavaria-based CSU put pressure on Kohl to harness the reunification movement.
- Something needed to be done to limit the growing refugee crisis. If the exodus continued, West Germany's welfare system would be in danger of collapse.
- Kohl faced elections in 1990. His poll standing was low. Politically, he could not afford to be seen as apathetic towards the East German crisis.

Kohl's problems

If Kohl was to deliver unification, he knew he would have his work cut out to convert a powerful number of opposition voices, both at home and abroad.

Left-wing opinion

Left-wing opinion in Germany was opposed to a Western-led, capitalist take-over of the East.

The East German government

On 13 November, a new leadership assumed power in East Germany. The government was led by Lothar de Maizière of the East German CDU, with Hans Modrow, a moderate SED reformer, as Prime Minister. The new leaders opposed a Western take-over. They hoped to find a 'third way' which would ensure the survival of a separate, model socialist East German state.

Soviet policy

Gorbachev, the Russian leader, while unwilling to intervene in East German internal affairs, was anxious to slow down the process of reunification. He was under fire from the old guard in the USSR who were deeply suspicious of his attempts both to reform Communism and to allow freedom to the USSR's satellite states.

Western opposition

Britain and France, despite their long public support for German reunification, privately warned US President **George Bush** that they opposed any swift process of unification. Margaret Thatcher, the British Prime Minister, told Gorbachev that Britain did not want German reunification. Germany's neighbours, particularly Poland, were also worried about any revival of Germany as a potentially expansionist great power.

Add the context

Below is a sample exam question with the accompanying source. Having read the question and the source, complete the following activity.

> Assess the value of Source 1 for revealing Chancellor Kohl's and George Bush's attitudes to German unification and the approaches of the two men to the process of bringing about unification. Explain your answer, using the source, the information given about its origin and your own knowledge about the historical content.

First, look for aspects of the source that refer to events and/or discussions that were going on around the time that the source was written. Underline the key phrases and write a brief description of the context in the margin next to the source. Draw an arrow from the key phrase to the context. Try and find three at least key phrases from the source.

Tip: look at the information above the source. You should contextualise this too. Pay particular attention to the date on which the source was written.

SOURCE 1

Letter from Chancellor Helmut Kohl to President George Bush, 28 November 1989. The letter demonstrates the extent to which Chancellor Kohl and President Bush were in constant (and friendly) contact in 1989–90. As well as writing, they frequently spoke on the telephone. Records of the correspondence were carefully preserved in the USA.

Dear George,

Thank you for your telephone request for information on the German situation for your upcoming meeting with General Secretary Gorbachev in Malta. I welcome this. This is a great sign of German–American friendship and partnership ...

The historical reform process we are currently experiencing in East and Central Europe is not only proceeding in the direction of Western values – free self-determination, democracy, private enterprise – but is also being carried out by the people themselves. That is why attempts to steer these reform developments from above or to channel or limit the movement of the people fail to meet the demands of this historical epoch.

... The issue that General Secretary Gorbachev will in all likelihood address – warding off of all destabilisation, increasing stability through reform – should be handled from this perspective.

Towards these goals, I would like to recommend full and complete agreement – in my name as well. The same goes for your assurance that America greets these reforms – and not as an opponent looking for an advantage, but rather as a people that offers support.

That is why it is important to establish with General Secretary Gorbachev the definition of both concepts. Contrary to what some Eastern propaganda still claims, destabilisation does not come from Western influence or an invasion from the West. Its source is more from an awakening after many decades of violent oppressive conflict (for example, ethnic conflict), or from the rejection of reforms and the subsequent reaction – or flight – of the people.

... Stability means stable development of reforms that guarantee the self-determination of the people – in the words of Gorbachev, 'freedom of choice' – that allows citizens a democratic stake in the political developments in their country, and open to the people a tangible future outlook in their homeland. In short: as in 1776, it is about life, liberty, and the pursuit of happiness!

Last but not least, stability means a positive foreign policy environment, especially dynamic progress in disarmament and arms control.

... The most important decisions over stability or destabilisation will be made by the countries in Central and East Europe. The duty of the West ... must be to support the ongoing reform process from the outside.

Rush to unity

Kohl's support for unification

In a surprise move, the USSR in late November 1989 informed Kohl that it favoured some form of German federation. Kohl decided to act.

Kohl's Ten-Point Plan

On 28 November 1989, Kohl announced a Ten-Point Plan, outlining a five-year process toward a German confederation based on economic unity and free elections in East Germany. Most West Germans supported his proposal. So did US President Bush. However, the USSR was critical: Kohl's plan went further than the loose confederation it had proposed.

Acceleration

On 19 December Kohl met GDR caretaker leader Modrow in Dresden. He was greeted by hundreds of thousands of rapturous people chanting 'Helmut', 'Deutschland' and 'unity'. This convinced Kohl that unification was possible and desirable in a shorter period that he had envisaged.

The situation in East Germany

In December 1989 the GDR's parliament (*Volkskammer*) eliminated the SED's monopoly of power. But East Germany was still in a state of near anarchy and economic meltdown as tens of thousands of people moved to West Germany. The GDR government now agreed that elections for a national assembly should take place on 18 March, two months earlier than planned.

On 1 February Kohl met leaders of the East German CDU and the parties which looked to ally with it. These parties formed the Alliance for Germany.

The international situation

- In February Kohl met Gorbachev in Moscow. Gorbachev, aware that the USSR was dependent on West German economic aid, declared: 'The German people must decide for themselves which path they choose to follow.'
- President Bush continued to encourage reunification.

- In order to limit the concerns among Germany's neighbours, Kohl spoke of German unity within the context of the European Union, stressing German and European unity as one and the same.

Currency reform

Kohl declared that the *Deutschmark* would be introduced in East Germany if the Alliance for Germany was successful in the March elections. Economic experts claimed this would have disastrous consequences. But Kohl insisted that the promise of currency reform would aid the Alliance for Germany politically and that immediate political considerations were more important than longer-term economic considerations.

18 March 1990 election

There were roughly three political groupings in East Germany:
- The Party of Democratic Socialism (PDS), the former SED, wanted the continuation of a separate GDR.
- *Bündnis* 90 wanted to retain elements of GDR separatism: it feared that Western consumerism would destroy the East's socialist achievements.
- The Alliance for Germany, the SPD and the Free Democrats supported unity. But they disagreed on aspects of process: the Alliance and the Democrats favoured the fastest route (unification under Article 23 of the Basic Law); the SPD favoured a new constitution – a slower, more complicated process.

The election result was a triumph for Kohl and unification. The Alliance won 48 per cent of the vote, the SPD 21.9 per cent, the Free Democrats 5.3 per cent, the PDS 16.4 per cent and *Bündnis 90* 2.9 per cent. The turn-out was an astonishing 93.4 per cent.

CDU leader de Maizière was eager to create a national government. Böhme, East German SPD chairman, opposed joining a grand coalition. But revelations that Böhme had been employed by the Stasi led to his disgrace. His successor Markus Merkel, although opposed to fast-track unification, agreed to join de Maizière's coalition.

Simple essay style

Below is a sample exam-style question. Use your own knowledge and the information on the opposite page to produce a plan for this question. Choose four general points and provide three pieces of specific information to support each general point. Once you have planned your essay, write the introduction and conclusion for the essay. The introduction should list the points to be discussed in the essay. The conclusion should summarise the key points and justify which point was the most important.

> How significant was the role of Chancellor Kohl in the rush to unification between November 1989 and March 1990?

You're the examiner

Below are a sample exam question and a paragraph written in answer to the question. Read the paragraph and the mark scheme provided on page 111. Describe which level you would award the paragraph. Write the level below, along with a justification for your choice.

> 'The East Germans, rather than Chancellor Kohl, led the "rush to unification" between November 1989 and March 1990.' How far do you agree with this statement?

In many respects Chancellor Kohl was taken by surprise at the speed of events in East Germany in November 1989, events over which he had little control. The fall of the Berlin Wall, the growing number of East Germans flocking to the West and the need to boost his low poll ratings (given there were parliamentary elections in Germany in 1990), forced Kohl to act. His actions were far more those of an opportunist than those of a visionary statesman. On 28 November he tried to take the initiative by announcing his Ten-Point Plan. He did so without consulting his FDP coalition partners or any of West Germany's allies. This plan outlined a tentative five-year process towards a German confederation. As early as mid-December 1989 it was apparent that the timescale was hopelessly wrong. Events in East Germany were again forcing Kohl's hand. He was following not leading.

Level:

Mark:

Reason for choosing this level and this mark:

_____

_____

German unity

Economic unity

Monetary and economic union was the first step to political union.

The Currency Union Treaty

On 18 May 1990 the East and West German governments signed the Currency Union Treaty (which was to take effect on 1 July 1990).

- The *Deutschmark* replaced the (almost worthless) East German mark as the official currency of East Germany.
- Wages and pensions were henceforth to be paid in German marks at par with the East German currency.
- Meanwhile, the FRG would provide massive loans to cover GDR pensions and unemployment benefits.

At the same time, many other FRG laws came into force in the GDR. This created a suitable framework for a political union by diminishing the huge gap between the two existing political, social and economic systems.

Political unity

Overcoming international barriers

In March the USSR insisted that a unified Germany as a member of NATO was unacceptable, as was the idea of unification under Article 23. But in May Moscow, in desperate need of financial assistance, turned to West Germany for help. Kohl immediately granted 5,000 million marks on the clear understanding that concessions were expected on the outstanding issues with respect to German unification. Gorbachev, whose political survival was dependent on FRG economic support, was prepared to pay the price. Gorbachev and Kohl met in mid-July. Gorbachev, in return for even more financial aid, agreed in principle to a united Germany in NATO.

The 'Two Plus Four' Treaty

This agreement was the final peace treaty negotiated between West Germany and the GDR (the 'Two') and the powers that occupied Germany in 1945: the USSR, Britain, France and the USA (the 'Four').

- The four Allied powers renounced all their rights in Germany, allowing a united Germany to become a sovereign state.
- Soviet troops would withdraw from Germany by the end of 1994.
- Germany agreed to limitations on its armed forces, promised to keep former East Germany a nuclear weapon-free zone, confirmed its 1945 borders and renounced any future territorial claims beyond those borders.

The treaty, agreed in September 1990, cleared the way for German unification.

The German Unification Treaty

Through the summer the two German states negotiated a German Unification Treaty. On 23 August the *Volkskammer* voted overwhelmingly for unification with the FRG under Article 23 of the Basic Law. The Unification Treaty was formally signed in Berlin on 31 August. On 20 September the Treaty was approved by large majorities in the *Bundestag* (447–47) and in the *Volkskammer* (299–80).

The Day of German Unity

On 3 October 1990, Germany was officially reunited. East Germany joined the FRG as five new states. Unification was not a merger that created a third state out of two. West Germany, in effect, absorbed East Germany. 3 October – the 'Day of German Unity' – was henceforth a national holiday.

Conclusion

Kohl, by seizing the opportunities offered to him, had triumphed. His accomplishments, not least convincing Gorbachev that a united Germany would not be a threat, and realising (faster than most) that a quick solution was essential if chaos was to be avoided, were considerable.

Nevertheless, he was aided by the favourable international circumstances, especially:

- the USSR's decline in power
- Hungary's decision to open its borders to East German refugees
- President Bush's consistent support.

! Mind map

Use the information on the opposite page to add detail to the mind map. This should assist your understanding as to how German unity finally came about in 1990.

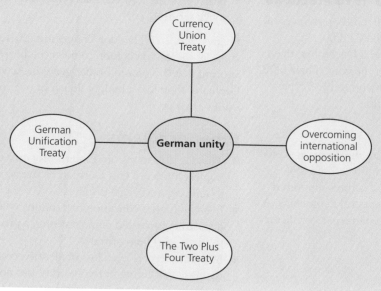

! Complete the paragraph ⓐ

Below are a sample exam-style question and a paragraph written in answer to the question. The paragraph contains a point and specific examples, but lacks a concluding explanatory link back to the question. Complete the paragraph, adding the link in the space provided.

'The Two Plus Four Treaty was the most important of all the treaties agreed in 1990.' How far do you agree with statement?

The Two Plus Four Treaty was vital. Germany could not be unified until the four victorious Allied powers of 1945 accepted the fact. The USSR was the nation most likely to oppose unification. But Mikhail Gorbachev, the Soviet leader, by mid-1990 accepted the necessity of unification. He struck a hard bargain for his support. Chancellor Kohl had to agree to domestic troop reductions, to provide considerable financial and technical aid to the USSR and pay for the removal of Soviet troops from former GDR territory. Thus, in September 1990 the Two Plus Four Treaty was agreed. The four Allied powers renounced all their rights in Germany while the still two Germanies confirmed the 1945 borders and renounced any future territorial claims beyond those existing borders.

_____

_____

Problems of transition

The political situation

The October and December 1990 elections

- Elections held in the five formerly GDR provinces on 14 October were a triumph for the CDU.
- In the *Bundestag* elections, held on 2 December, the CDU/CSU won 43.8 per cent of the vote. Their FDP allies won 11 per cent. The SPD won only 33.5 per cent. Kohl continued as Chancellor.

The German capital

There was disagreement about where the German capital should be. Some favoured Berlin: Bonn seemed too remote from the five new provinces. Others supported Bonn, capital of Germany's first successful democracy. A vote in the *Bundestag* in 1991 resulted in a narrow victory for Berlin.

Economic issues

East German problems

The East's industry was antiquated and its entire infrastructure decrepit. Experts estimated that only one-third of East German enterprises were potentially profitable. East Germany also had huge ecological problems. Air pollution levels, for example, were seven times higher than in the West. With the introduction of a capitalist market economy, nearly a fifth of East Germans found themselves unemployed. The government tried to relieve the situation with make-work programmes, by encouraging early retirement, and by providing funds to save firms from bankruptcy – to little avail.

The currency union

The 1:1 currency conversion rate was economically damaging. Problems occurred in the run-up to reunion. Westerners travelled to the East to snap up bargains, leading to shortages. Meanwhile East German shops began to fill with Western goods at prices Easterners could not afford. Many soon felt worse off due to higher prices for food and services.

Mounting costs

Kohl's administration underestimated the costs of reunification.

- West Germany took on the GDR's burden of debt, estimated to be over 600,000 million marks.

- West Germans had to support their unproductive Eastern compatriots, including providing funding for nearly half the East German population dependent on social services.

Finance minister Theodor Waigel initially refused to consider increased taxation to meet the horrendous costs, arguing that this would hinder growth. Accordingly Germany soon had a budget deficit of over one million, million marks.

Other problems

- The decision to restore Eastern property to previous owners hindered East German recovery, slowing rebuilding until legal disputes were resolved.
- In some higher education institutions whole academic departments needed democratising, a process that led to many staff being fired.
- Many Easterners felt a loss of identity, commonly expressed as 'living in two worlds, but not feeling at home in either one'. Easterners resented Westerners who thought they knew better. Westerners could not understand why Easterners were not more grateful.
- Investigations into those who had collaborated with the Stasi caused dissension, paralleling the denazification disputes after 1945.
- Excessive expectations among Easterners, coupled with widespread resentment among Westerners of the financial sacrifices expected of them, caused domestic conflict which permeated Germany's political agenda.

Reunification success

In many respects reunification proved successful.

Political success

The whole of Germany now became a smooth-functioning, parliamentary democracy. Fears that a united Germany might return to right-wing nationalism proved unjustified. The new Germany remained firmly embedded in the Atlantic Alliance and in the confederation of states that became the European Union.

Economic success

Germany continued to be economically successful, an industrial powerhouse. Most former East Germans soon had a much higher standard of living.

Spectrum of significance

Below are a sample exam-style question and a list of general points which could be used to answer the question. Use your own knowledge and the information on the opposite page to reach a judgement about the importance of these general points to the question posed. Write numbers on the spectrum to indicate their relative importance. Having done this, write a brief justification of your placement, explaining why some of these factors are more important than others. The resulting diagram could form the basis of an essay plan.

To what extent were Germany's problems just beginning after unification in 1990?

1   The political situation

2   The problem of the German capital

3   East German industrial backwardness

4   The currency union

5   Mounting costs

6   Divisions between East and West

← Not a major problem   Major problem →

Develop the detail   a

Below are a sample exam-style question and the paragraph written in answer to the question. The paragraph contains a limited amount of detail. Annotate the paragraph to add additional detail to the answer.

To what extent was German unification a political triumph and an economic disaster?

One of the economic problems was the cost of unification. This mainly fell on what had been West Germany. The West Germans took over East Germany's huge debts. They also had to support East Germany's antiquated economy and pay for its social services. The costs were astronomic.

Exam focus

Below are an exam-style source-based question and a model answer. Read it and the comments around it.

Assess the value of Source 1 for revealing Chancellor Helmut Kohl's and US President George Bush's attitudes to German unification and the approaches of the two men to the process of bringing about unification. Explain your answer, using the source, the information given about its origin and your own knowledge about the historical content.

SOURCE 1

An extract from a telephone conversation between Chancellor Helmut Kohl and US President George Bush, initiated by Kohl on 13 February 1990. The American government recorded President Bush's telephone conversations, many of which are now available to historians. Kohl had recently visited both East Germany and the USSR, where he had met Soviet leader Gorbachev.

Chancellor Kohl: [East German] Prime Minister [Hans] Modrow is here today. The situation continues to be dramatic. Between the 1st of January and today, 80,000 have come from the GDR to the Federal Republic. That is why I suggested a monetary union and an economic community ...

Your support is invaluable.

Let me say a few words about my talks in Moscow. Gorbachev was very relaxed ... But the problems he faces are enormous – nationalities, the food supply situation – and I do not see a light at the end of the tunnel yet.

You know the text we published jointly on the German Question. It was highly satisfactory. We will go in that direction now, and in a parallel way policy ... At Camp David [a place where US Presidents often hold meetings], there is one thing we will have to discuss thoroughly: the future of NATO and the Warsaw Pact. I feel we will find a solution, but it will be hard work. I told Gorbachev again that the neutralisation of Germany is out of the question for me.

The President: Did he acquiesce or just listen? How did he react?

Chancellor Kohl: My impression is that this is a subject about which they want to negotiate, but that we can win that point in negotiations. The modalities [methods/style] will be important but I do believe we can find a solution.

The President: We must find a solution. The Camp David meeting will be very important, and I am delighted you are able to come. When I heard your comments from Moscow and heard that Mr Gorbachev had removed a long-standing obstacle to unification, I was thinking of you as a friend. It must have been an emotional moment for you. The German people certainly want to be together.

Chancellor Kohl: That is quite true. This is a great moment.

The President: We have been supporting your stated position that NATO membership will be appropriate. We won't move away from that but we do need to talk and see where we need to be more flexible and where we need to be more firm.

The source provides an excellent view of the thoughts and attitudes of President Bush and Chancellor Kohl on a number of issues with regard to German unification in mid-February 1990. Given that the two men were on very close terms, it is probably safe to assume they were not lying to each other. The telephone conversation, therefore, probably tells us what they were thinking on a number of issues, for example discussions with Gorbachev, NATO and their forthcoming meeting at Camp David in the USA. Presumably Bush was aware that the telephone conversation was being recorded for posterity. Was Kohl? Would he have said the same if he knew or didn't know? That is a moot point. What is certain is that both men seem to have built up a close relationship and were prepared to act as one. The fact that they were speaking together on the telephone is itself an indication of their friendship and willingness to co-operate. The unification of Germany is usually regarded as resulting from the actions of the East German people. To a large extent, East German actions in late 1989 began the process. But as this source points out, by February 1990 Bush and Kohl, both of whom had been taken by surprise by the speed of events, were trying to control matters. Their joint planning was to be of considerable significance in 1990.

Quite an impressive introduction which raises some issues about the source's credibility and about the importance of the Bush–Kohl relationship.

By February 1990 German unification was advancing at a pace that few had imagined. Kohl and Bush were both committed to the 'rush to unity'. They knew that the real stumbling block was Mikhail Gorbachev, the USSR leader. Gorbachev in 1987 had talked about unification being a hundred years in the future. But events in East Germany in November and December 1989 had convinced the Soviet leader (by January 1990) that unification was inevitable. On 10 February he met Kohl in Moscow and told him that 'the Germans themselves have to make their own choice' – a strong indication that he accepted unity. But Soviet blessing for a united Germany (which Kohl immediately publicised) did not solve the thorny problem of what role a united Germany would play in the European security system, in particular whether it would be a member of NATO. It seemed certain that the USSR was opposed to a united Germany becoming a member of NATO. Instead, Soviet leaders envisaged Germany becoming a neutral power in central Europe, as did some East Germans. This issue could well get in the way of the 'rush to unity'. That said, by early 1990 Gorbachev was not controlling events: he was being driven by them. The enormous problems he faced on a number of fronts limited his room for manoeuvre and gave Kohl, with Bush's backing, the opportunity to speed up the process of unification.

This paragraph is essentially one about context. It shows good understanding of the situation in Germany and internationally in February 1990.

Kohl's telephone conversation with Bush came soon after his return from Moscow. The conversation was, in many respects, a report by Kohl on recent developments, which continued to move on apace. Kohl says more in the extract than Bush. He first informs the President about the exodus of 80,000 East Germans to West Germany since 1 January 1990. Given the economic consequences for East Germany, Kohl informs Bush that he is proposing a 'monetary union' and an 'economic community' between East and West Germany.

A paragraph which simply paraphrases the source.

After thanking Bush for his continued support, Kohl describes his meeting with Gorbachev on 10–11 February in Moscow. Gorbachev, he says, was 'relaxed', despite the immense problems he faced. Kohl mentions the nationalities problem in the USSR and the food supply situation. (He might have added its economic problems, the situation across much of Eastern Europe, and the fact that Gorbachev faced increasing opposition from the 'old guard' in the USSR, who were dismayed at the break-up of the Soviet empire in Eastern Europe.) After telling Bush that he is very happy with the joint declaration they made on the German Question, he goes on to discuss the meeting he will have with Bush at Camp David in the USA (on 24 February). The future of NATO will be an important part of their agenda. Kohl is upbeat about their chances of finding a solution to the problem. He thinks Gorbachev is prepared to negotiate and that he and Bush can 'win' the negotiations.

Bush congratulates Kohl on the fact that German unification now has Soviet backing. The President's main concern was to ensure that a united Germany remained within NATO. He is interested in how Gorbachev reacted to the NATO issue at their meeting on 10–11 February. He tells Kohl that the USA 'won't move' on its NATO position. But he suggests that he and Kohl will need to think about how they might discuss the issue with Gorbachev. Bush, it seems, has no wish to force the Soviet leader into a corner.

The approaches of the two men to the process of unification seem clear. Kohl is determined to press on at full speed. He is already talking of some form of currency union with East Germany. He seems to be confident of the relationship he has built up with Gorbachev. He is optimistic that Gorbachev will be flexible, even on the NATO front. Kohl had good reasons for his optimism. He does not say this in the source but he was aware that Gorbachev was increasingly reliant on West German money. This gave Kohl potentially huge influence over Gorbachev.

Bush, unlike Margaret Thatcher of Britain and François Mitterrand of France (both of whom feared destabilisation of the existing order and a German-dominated Europe), was totally supportive of German reunification – provided the united Germany remained a full member of NATO. Although he does not say this in the telephone conversation, he had met the Soviet leader face-to-face in Malta in December 1989 and had built up a reasonably strong personal relationship. The problem for Bush, again not stated in the source, was that the USA had many other issues with the USSR apart from Germany. These included arms reduction, the situation in Central America and bringing an end to the Cold War. The USA's position on the situation in Germany and Eastern Europe was remarkably consistent. From the spring of 1989 it had pursued the twin goals of liberating Eastern Europe from the USSR and reunifying Germany. At the same time, it did its best not to undermine or endanger Gorbachev's position in the USSR.

Yet more paraphrasing. In fairness, some paraphrasing is certainly necessary. The candidate also links the source to his/her own knowledge in places.

Bush is now paraphrased.

This paragraph might have been better integrated with the paragraphs paraphrasing Kohl.

This paragraph could have been integrated with the paragraph paraphrasing Bush.

To 'listen into' a conversation between Kohl and Bush is clearly fascinating. Nevertheless, the source has limitations. Most of what the two leaders say, they had said before in much longer written communications. Indeed, they say nothing that cannot be found elsewhere and nothing here that was particularly significant. Nevertheless, historians of almost any period would give their right arm for a direct, almost face-to-face conversation between two key Western figures on a major issue – in this case German unification.

German unity possibly came even faster than the two men envisaged in February 1990. East German elections in March 1990 saw parties committed to union, particularly the CDU, triumph. A currency union, hinted at by Kohl in the source, was signed in May. By July 1990 Gorbachev, even more dependent on West German aid, agreed to German unification, even if the new German state was part of NATO. In return Kohl agreed to pay huge sums to support Russian soldiers who would remain in the former East Germany for four years. The Two Plus Four Treaty was signed in September and the new united Germany came into official existence on 3 October 1990. This could not have happened without the situation in East Germany (which in some ways reflected the situation across Eastern Europe as the USSR's power waned). Nor could it have happened without the – often – grudging support of Gorbachev. But as the source makes clear, the consistent support of Bush for German unification and the fact that he and Kohl were prepared to work together for very similar goals were also crucial.

> The paragraph is a bit short but does make one or two important, if basic, points.

> This concluding paragraph shows excellent contextual knowledge but says next to nothing about the source.

This answer is probably just about a Level 4 – on the strength of its contextual knowledge and the fact that it is very well written. Its main failing is the fact that it fails to examine the source in sufficient depth. There is room for more analysis, more evaluation, more judgement and more inference.

Moving from a Level 4 to Level 5

The exam focus essay at the end of Section 3 (pages 49–50) provided a Level 5 essay. The essay here achieves a Level 4. Read both essays and the comments provided. Make a list of the additional features required to push a Level 4 essay into Level 5.

6 Social change in Germany and West Germany, 1871–1990

Social change and prosperity, 1871–1933

German society in 1871

- A few nobles owned vast estates.
- The **bourgeoisie** was expanding.
- Most Germans were agricultural workers.
- Growing industry swelled the ranks of the proletariat.

Bismarck's introduction of pensions and health insurance

Bismarck loathed socialism (see page 12). Hoping to wean the working classes from socialism, he introduced the Sickness Insurance Act (1883), the Accident Insurance Act (1884) and the Old Age and Disability Act (1889). While failing to stop the rise of socialism, Bismarck's 'state socialism' measures laid the foundations of the German welfare state.

Social trends in Germany, 1880–1914

The German population rose to 68 million by 1914 – 60 per cent higher than in 1871. Improvements in hygiene and medical care resulted in Germans living longer.

The growth of the urban working class

The 'flight' from the countryside to the towns built up speed after 1880. By 1914 nearly two-thirds of Germans lived in towns. By 1907 Berlin had over 2 million inhabitants, 60 per cent of whom had been born outside the city.

The decline of the peasantry

While there were still 7 million agricultural workers in 1914, many felt they were outcasts, disadvantaged with regard to pay, education provision and medical care.

The urban working classes

Between 1885 and 1913 wages in Germany rose and working hours fell by a third. While industrial employment seemed attractive to rural workers, urban living and working conditions remained poor. Most workers lived in overcrowded housing and spent much of their income on food. Insecurity, particularly with regard to employment, was endemic. Such conditions encouraged the rise of labour movements. By 1914 there were 3 million trade union members.

The lower middle class

White-collar workers – minor civil servants, foremen, clerks, shopkeepers – were expanding rapidly. Such men, along with skilled craftsmen, continued the strong **artisan** tradition in Germany. They considered themselves above, and were generally better paid than, most of the urban working classes. Lower-middle-class families often had greater aspirations for their children than working-class families.

The bourgeoisie

Middle-class families were increasingly wealthy. They could afford fine houses, holidays and servants. A few great industrialists had more wealth than many noble families.

Society in the 1920s

While there was some social mobility after the First World War, society was riven by class antagonisms in the 1920s.

The élite

Five per cent of the population were in the economic élite – industrialists, financiers and landowners. The fall in agricultural prices post-1922 meant that landowning nobles declined in wealth and influence.

The middle classes

The middle class made up at least a third of the population, ranging from doctors, lawyers and professors at the top to increasing numbers of white-collar workers at the bottom.

The working classes

The working classes comprised over half the population. They were far from united. Wages varied from industry to industry and there were important regional differences. Farm labourers, still a third of the population, had little in common with industrial workers.

Standard of living

For most of the 1920s, the standard of living of most Germans was rising. Wages rose in real terms every year from 1924 to 1929. There were also improvements in the provision of social welfare, medical care and housing.

The **Great Depression** changed everything. By 1932 there were 8 million Germans unemployed, totally overwhelming the welfare system.

Complete the paragraph **a**

Below are a question and a paragraph written as part of the answer to this question. The paragraph contains a point and a concluding explanatory link back to the question, but lacks examples. Complete the paragraph, adding examples in the space provided.

To what extent was there increased social mobility in German society in the years 1871–1933?

In 1871 most Germans lived and worked on the land. By 1914, however, the situation had changed.

_____

_____

Thus, by 1914 most Germans belonged to the urban working class — the proletariat. This was the main social development in the period from 1871 to 1914.

Simple essay style

Below is a question. Use your own knowledge and the information on the opposite page to produce a plan for this question. Choose four general points and provide three pieces of specific information to support each general point. Once you have planned your essay, write the introduction and conclusion for the essay. The introduction should list the points to be discussed in the essay. The conclusion should summarise the key points and justify which point was the most important.

'The main social development in Germany in the years 1871–1933 was the rise of the urban working class.' How far do you agree with this statement?

Tip: this question can be answered by including the information on page 82 with that on page 84.

Social change and prosperity, 1933–90

Nazi society

Adolf Hitler came to power in 1933. His government, the Third Reich, claimed to be creating a new and better kind of society, a 'people's community' (*Volksgemeinschaft*), in which class divisions would cease.

Standards of living

The Nazis promised Germans 'a better deal'. Economic recovery ensured that, on balance, they were able to keep this promise.

- Wages improved steadily after 1933. Benefits for industrial workers also included such things as improved canteens, education courses and subsidised tourism.
- Social welfare programmes were improved.

Social mobility

Hitler aimed to promote social mobility. Some progress was made on this front. Workers, for example, were encouraged to acquire new skills and offered generous incentives for advancement. Given the brief period of Nazi rule, long-term changes scarcely had time to take effect.

A people's community?

While many Germans do seem to have felt an increased sense of comradeship:

- class identities were not eradicated
- the Third Reich was a dictatorship, prepared to use terror against those who did not conform to its standards
- many Germans – Jews, homosexuals, Gypsies and the 'asocial' – were excluded from the national community (see page 62).

Germany, 1945–49

Defeat in the Second World War ended Nazi rule. The years 1945–49 were years of desperate poverty for most Germans. Their land, homes and property lay in ruins. Initially, the Allied treatment of Germans was not benevolent. The Russians had many scores to settle while the Americans, British and French blamed the Germans for the Second World War and the Holocaust. But American and British attitudes changed relatively quickly. This was largely due to:

- humanitarian concerns
- the realisation that German economic and political reconstruction was vital to counter the threat of Communism.

West Germany post-1949

The West German economic miracle after 1949 led to enormous advances in material well-being for many in the 1950s and 60s. Wages almost doubled between 1949 and 1955 while a generous health and social welfare system was an integral part of the social market economy. There was greater social mobility and some redistribution of wealth as the rich were taxed to help the poor. Social stratification and class differences became outwardly less visible and there was an absence of serious social tensions for most of the 1950s and 60s. By the 1950s the landed élite and the peasantry, both in slow decline since the late nineteenth century, had essentially disappeared.

Social tensions in the 1950s

Some historians claim there was a superficial quality to life in the 1950s as West Germans focused on work and material enrichment.

- Few Germans openly discussed the Nazi years.
- The war created a communication gap between wives and husbands, neither volunteering their experiences of home and battle front beyond banal generalisations.
- Relatively cramped housing conditions and long hours at work added to family strain.

Young versus old

In the late 1960s a new generation, angry at the seemingly bland conformity of society, took to the streets to voice its complaints. Idealistic youngsters protested against the 'bourgeois materialism' of their parents. By the 1970s West German youth had developed a distinctive political voice, espousing green and anti-capitalist issues.

Immigration tensions

West Germany's economic success resulted in an influx of foreign workers, mainly from southern Europe and Turkey. By 1990 West Germany's population of foreign workers and their families totalled 6 million. There was a significant gap between the relatively poor immigrants and the growing number of university-educated, wealthy Germans at the top of the social structure.

Spectrum of significance

Below are a question and a list of general points which could be used to answer the question. Use your own knowledge and the information on the opposite page to reach a judgement about the importance of these general points to the question posed. Write numbers on the spectrum below to indicate their relative importance. Having done this, write a brief justification of your placement, explaining why some of these factors are more important than others. The resulting diagram could form the basis of an essay plan.

To what extent was there increased social mobility in German and West German society in the years 1871–1990?

1 The flight from the countryside post-1871

2 The rise of white-collar workers post-1871

3 The rise in standard of living in the 1920s

4 The impact of the Great Depression

5 Nazi *Volksgemeinschaft*

6 Nazi social mobility schemes

7 The situation in 1945

8 German prosperity in the 1950s and 60s

9 The youth 'revolt' of the 1960s

10 The impact of foreign immigration

←————————————————————————————→

Social stability   **Social mobility**

 Develop the detail　　　　　　　　　　　　　a

Below are a question and a paragraph written as part of an answer to this question. The paragraph contains a limited amount of detail. Annotate the paragraph to add additional detail to the answer.

To what extent was there increased social mobility in German society in the years 1871–1990?

One of Hitler's aims in 1933 was to create a 'people's community', uniting all ethnic Germans. He also hoped to promote social mobility. Some progress was made towards achieving this goal. More might have been done but for the outbreak of the Second World War.

The changing role of women in Germany, 1871–1933

REVISED

The situation in 1871

In 1871 Germany assigned unequal roles to men and women. Women were seen, and saw themselves, as home-makers – a view disseminated by the Church and the growing publishing industry. Women were denied the same social and political rights as men. They could not vote or even own property. While middle-class married women were not expected to work, many working-class wives had no option but to do so in order to provide basic provision for their families.

The position of women, 1880–1914

While Germany still had 1.25 million female domestic servants in 1914, this was a declining share of the labour force. More women were working in better-paid industrial or clerical jobs.

There were growing opportunities for unmarried middle-class women.
- Female teacher training expanded from the 1890s.
- Women were prominent in the expanding welfare professions like nursing and social work.
- In 1899 women were permitted to acquire medical qualifications after long male resistance.

However, male hostility to female emancipation remained deep-rooted. Few women went to university and women remained inferior in law. Abortion was illegal and a double morality persisted in sexual morality. Men could have mistresses but women were ostracised for committing adultery.

Nevertheless, by 1914 women were becoming more publicly active, at work, in charities, even in politics. This was particularly true of middle-class women, many of whom joined the Federation of German Women's Organisations set up in 1894. But more working-class women joined trade unions and the SDP.

The impact of the First World War

- After the outbreak of war in 1914, women helped Germany cope with its labour shortage in agriculture and industry, many doing jobs traditionally done by men.
- Some women involved themselves in politics. Rosa Luxemburg, for example, was one of the leaders of the Spartacist revolt (see page 28).
- In 1919 women gained equal rights under the Weimar constitution. All women over the age of 20 could vote. Given the losses of men in the war, women were a majority of the electorate.

Women's role in the 1920s

The media propagated the idea of the 'new woman'. Magazines displayed images of cigarette-smoking, short-skirted young women in bars or on the sports field. The 'new woman' image had some basis in reality.
- More women found work in new occupations, especially in public services, shops and factories.
- Many young women spent their leisure at sports clubs, dance halls and in cinemas.
- Women had more sexual independence.
- Left-wing women campaigned for the reform of the abortion law and established a network of contraceptive clinics.

Nevertheless, the 'new woman' was something of a myth.
- The proportion of women who worked outside the home remained roughly the same as before 1914 – as did their type of work.
- Although many women had been employed in 'men's jobs' during the war, these better-paid jobs were taken back by men after 1918.
- Social attitudes to women's role in society remained conservative. Married women were not expected to work outside the home. Those who did – the *Doppelverdienerinnen* – became a source of controversy.

Use the information on the opposite page to add detail to the mind map below. This should increase your understanding of the changing role of women in the years 1871–1933.

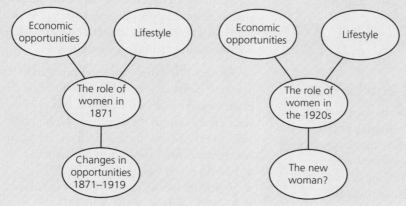

Below are a question and a paragraph written as part of an answer to this question. Why does the paragraph not get into Level 4? Once you have identified the mistake, rewrite the paragraph so that it displays the qualities of Level 4. The mark scheme on pages 111–12 will help you.

To what extent did women's role change in Germany in the years 1871–1933?

In 1919 German women gained formally equal rights under the Weimar constitution. In the 1920s a growing number of women worked in new areas of employment, especially in the civil service, in teaching, in shops and on assembly lines. The 'new woman' spent her leisure time in sports clubs, dance halls and cinemas. She also had more sexual independence.

The changing role of women, 1933–90

Women's role in Nazi Germany

Hitler believed women should be confined to their 'natural' roles as wives and mothers (see page 46).

Ironically, given Hitler's goals, the number of employed women increased in the late 1930s as labour shortage drew many females into work.

Women in the Second World War

In 1939 Hitler refused to authorise the mass conscription of women into the workforce. Although women played an important role in gathering the harvest, the numbers of women employed in industry actually decreased between 1939 and 1941. Wives of soldiers received enhanced welfare benefits to cover their husbands' absence.

However, from January 1943, all women aged between 17 and 45 were required to register for work, although there were exceptions for pregnant women, those with two or more children and farmers' wives. By 1945, 60 per cent of German workers were women and the upper age limit for compulsory work had been extended to 50. By 1945 nearly half a million women were working for the military in auxiliary roles. A similar number worked as voluntary nurses and in civilian aerial defence.

The post-war situation: new opportunities

Many women's lasting memories of the end of the war were of fear, scrounging for food and fuel and of finding themselves at the total mercy of the enemy. An estimated 2 million German women were raped by Soviet soldiers in 1945. (Between 150,000 and 200,000 'Russian babies' were born in the Soviet zone of Germany in 1945 and 1946.) In 1945 over a quarter of all houses in Germany were destroyed. Given the shortage of men, women set about the work of rebuilding Germany. While this provided women with huge challenges, it also gave them opportunities to prove themselves in jobs and roles previously undertaken by men.

Women's role in West Germany

The Basic Law (1949) declared that men and women were equal. But in the 1950s there was initially little change from the prevailing pre-war values of *Kinder, Kirche, Küche* (children, church, kitchen). Males were still considered the natural breadwinners.

In the mid-1960s this conformism began to shatter as young women, within the context of the broader generational revolt of the decade, began to demand emancipation from their perceived subservient gender role. The 1970s saw significant gains for women as a coherent women's movement blossomed.

- Abortion was legalised in 1976.
- Women achieved equal rights in marriage in 1977.
- In 1980 a federal office responsible for women's affairs was created.
- By the early 1980s the percentage of women going into higher education equalled male numbers.
- There were increasing employment opportunities for women.

Nevertheless, the persistence of a traditional patriarchal family and work structure continued. By 1987 women still only comprised ten per cent of *Bundestag* representatives.

Eliminate irrelevance

Below are a question and a paragraph written as part of an answer to this question. Read the paragraph and identify parts of the paragraph that are not directly relevant to the question. Draw a line through the information that is irrelevant and justify your deletions in the margin.

> To what extent did equal rights for women develop in Germany and West Germany in the years 1871–1990?

The Third Reich did little to encourage equal rights for women. Hitler and the Nazis were profoundly anti-feminist. They believed that women should be confined to their 'natural' roles as wives and mothers. Hitler, in particular, stressed the importance of Kinder, Kirche, Küche (children, church, kitchen). A major decline in the German birth rate in the 1920s led to fears that racial 'inferiors' might 'out-birth' the German 'master race'. Therefore a raft of measures were introduced to encourage German women to have more children. Abortion was prohibited and restrictions placed on the acquisition of contraceptives. Financial incentives were given to families which had large numbers of children. Mothers who had large families were held in esteem and given an award: the Mothers' Cross. Those who had four children got a bronze medal, those with five a silver medal and those with six or more a gold medal. Nazi birth-encouraging policies were successful. In 1936 there were 30 per cent more births than there had been in 1933. Ironically, given the regime's goals, the number of employed women actually increased after 1937. This was because the Nazi regime was doing well economically. Its efforts to produce 'guns' (for war) and 'butter' (an improved standard of living) meant there was a labour shortage. This drew many females into work. Hitler worried about this. He continued to believe that a woman's place was in the home. Given his views, little was done for equal rights for women between 1933 and 1939.

Introducing an argument

Below are a sample exam-style question, a list of key points to be made in the essay and a simple introduction and conclusion for the essay. Read the question, the plan and the introduction and conclusion. Rewrite the introduction and conclusion in order to develop an argument.

> To what extent did the role of women in Germany and West Germany change in the years 1871–1990?

Key points

- Women's role pre-1914
- The situation in the 1920s
- Nazi policy 1933–39
- The impact of the Second World War
- Women's role in West Germany in the 1950s
- Changes in the 1960s and 70s
- The situation by 1990

Introduction

While there is clear evidence to suggest that equal rights for women did develop in the years 1933–90, that progress was slow. Indeed, there was little progress until the 1970s and 80s.

Conclusion

Thus, by 1990 women had far more equality — especially economic opportunity — than they had in 1933. However, the move to equality was slow and women were still far from equal citizens in 1990.

Tip: this question can be answered by including the information on page 86 with that on page 88.

Exam focus

Below is a sample Section C essay. Read it and the comments around it.

To what extent did the years 1871–1990 see a consistent advance in the rights and opportunities of women in Germany and West Germany?

The period from 1871 to 1990 saw considerable changes in the rights and opportunities of German women. However, the advance towards female equality was far from consistent. While important changes occurred in some decades, in others relatively little progress was made. In the 1930s, for example, women actually lost rights and opportunities previously gained. It should be said that not all women supported the move to female equality. Many Germans – male and female – throughout the period 1871–1990 supported Hitler's notion of *Kinder, Kirche, Küche*. The strength of opposition to changes in women's role helps explain the inconsistency in the progress of female emancipation. Nevertheless, by 1990 women's role in German society was very different from what it had been in the 1870s.

The introduction focuses well on the set question and provides a guide of the likely direction the essay will take. It makes the good point that German women were split on the issue of female emancipation.

In 1871 Germany, like Europe generally, assigned decidedly unequal roles to men and women. Women were seen, and saw themselves, as home-makers. This view was disseminated by the Church (which was very influential) and by the growing publishing industry. Women were denied the same legal, social, economic and political rights as men. Few went to university. Many continued to have large families. Nevertheless, despite male (and some female) hostility to female emancipation, women became more publicly active, at work, in charities and even in politics. There were growing career opportunities for unmarried middle-class women in teaching, welfare professions and even medicine. Large numbers of middle-class women joined the Federation of German Women's Organisations, established in 1894. An increasing number of working-class women joined trade unions and were active in the SPD. Thus, some progress, albeit inconsistent, was made with regard to women's rights and opportunities prior to 1914.

A well-informed paragraph which establishes the situation in 1871 and examines some of the developments between 1871 and 1914. It displays good knowledge and good skills of analysis and synthesis. The last sentence also links back to the question.

The First World War helped the cause of German women's advancement (but not necessarily their happiness, given the huge loss of loved ones). Women assisted the war effort by undertaking work previously done by men. In 1919 the Weimar constitution granted women equal rights with men, including the right to vote. Given male losses in the war, the majority of voters were now women. Some women, following the lead of Rosa Luxemburg, involved themselves in politics. But generally women did not use their potential political power to great effect. Although more women were elected to the *Reichstag* than to the British Parliament or American Congress, politics in Germany in the 1920s was a largely male preserve. Female emancipation was thus by no means assured.

The paragraph does well to focus on the First World War, suggesting that the war was something of a catalyst in regard to women's role. However, the last three sentences suggest that female emancipation was not going to be plain sailing.

The role of women and the debate about their status was an important feature of Weimar society. The media propagated the idea of the 'new woman'. Illustrated magazines, for example, displayed illustrations of cigarette-smoking, short-skirted young women in bars or dance halls. The 'new woman' image had some basis in reality. More women worked in new areas of employment – in public services, shops and factories. More spent their leisure time in dance halls, at the cinema and in sports clubs. Women also had greater sexual independence. Abortion clinics were established and contraceptive advice given. However, the 'new woman' was not entirely the reality. The proportion of women who worked outside the home during the 1920s remained roughly the same as before 1914, as did their type of work. Women who had done (better-paid) 'men's jobs' during the First World War lost them after 1918. Social attitudes to women's role remained conservative. Most Germans, men and women alike, still considered married women's place was in the home. Nevertheless, female emancipation made considerable strides in the liberal climate of Weimar Germany.

A well-informed and well-balanced paragraph, well-geared to the question, which examines the situation in the 1920s and reaches a mini-conclusion.

The same could not be said about Nazi Germany. Hitler and the Nazis were profoundly anti-feminist. They believed women should be confined to their 'natural roles' as wives and mothers. A decline in the birth rate in the 1920s had led to fears that racial 'inferiors' would 'out-birth' Aryan Germans. A whole raft of policies was introduced to counter this trend. Abortion was prohibited and restrictions placed on contraception. Generous child allowances were provided while mothers who had large families were held in esteem. Nazi birth-encouraging policies were successful: in 1936 there were nearly a third more births than in 1933. Ironically, given Hitler's goals, the number of employed women increased in the late 1930s as labour shortage drew many females into work. Nevertheless, in 1939 Hitler refused to authorise the conscription of women into the workforce. Indeed, the numbers of women employed in industry decreased between 1939 and 1941. As the war turned against Germany, Nazi policy changed. From January 1943, all women aged between 17 and 45 were required to register for work. By 1945, 60 per cent of German workers were women and the upper age limit for compulsory work had been extended to 50. By 1945 nearly 500,000 women worked for the military in auxiliary roles. Thus, while there was a decline in the advance of female emancipation in Nazi Germany, the decline was not entirely consistent.

Given the shortage of men, women set about the work of rebuilding Germany after 1945. The Basic Law (1949) declared that men and women were equal. But in the 1950s there was initially little change from the prevailing pre-war values of *Kinder, Kirche, Küche*. Men were still seen as the natural breadwinners. In the mid-1960s this conformism began to shatter as young women began to demand emancipation from their perceived subservient role. The 1970s, in particular, saw significant gains for women as a coherent women's movement blossomed. Abortion was legalised in 1976. Women achieved equal rights in marriage in 1977. In 1980 a federal office responsible for women's affairs was created. By the mid-1980s the percentage of women going into higher education equalled male numbers. There were also better employment opportunities for women. Nevertheless, the traditional patriarchal family and work structure persisted.

Although feminists still had major battles to fight, women's role in German society by 1990 was very different from what it had been in the 1870s. By 1990 women were seen as equal to men, both in legal terms and politically. They had far greater opportunities, economically, socially and sexually. An advance had occurred. The advance was partly the result of battles fought by German women (and some men) and partly the result of Germany following world trends. But it had been a relatively slow and far from consistent advance. This was partly because many Germans of both sexes had opposed female equality. Given the strength of opposition, it is perhaps surprising that German women had managed to gain the rights and opportunities they possessed in 1990.

This paragraph, like the previous paragraphs, displays good skills of analysis and synthesis. Its final sentence is perceptive. Even the Third Reich was not totally consistent with regard to women's role and opportunities.

This paragraph covers 45 years. It can only skirt the surface of the advance towards female emancipation. But it does so quite effectively.

The conclusion very much ties in with the introduction and with the issues raised in the course of the essay. It displays consistent analysis.

This is a Level 5 essay. It is thorough and detailed, clearly engaging with the question and offering a balanced and carefully reasoned argument, which is sustained throughout the essay. It also shows good skills of analysis and synthesis.

Consolidation

This is a long and detailed essay. Arguably it is overlong. Without losing the overall argument of the essay, experiment with reducing its length by 100 words. This is a particularly useful exercise for trying to produce an essay which gets to the heart of the question without being overlong.

7 Economic change in Germany and West Germany, 1871–1990

Economic change, 1871–1933

Industrial growth and agricultural decline, 1871–1914

Between 1870 and 1914 Germany's industrial capacity increased eightfold. By 1914 Germany was Europe's industrial superpower. It was particularly successful in expanding 'new' industries – steel, electrical engineering, chemicals and automobiles.

Reasons for German industrial growth

- Germany's population growth (from 40 million in 1871 to 68 million in 1914) provided the market and the labour for an expanding economy.
- Germany possessed huge resources of coal and iron ore.
- Germany had an excellent education and transport system.
- German banks worked closely with industrial firms.
- The development of **cartels** promoted efficiency.

Agriculture

In 1888 agriculture's share of Germany's **gross national product** (GNP) had been about a half; by 1914 this had shrunk to under a quarter.

The First World War

Germany's strong economy enabled it to fight a four-year war. However:
- Poor harvests, shortage of chemicals for fertilisers (arising from the Allied naval blockade), and mass conscription led to serious food shortages.
- German governments paid for the war by printing money. This fuelled **inflation**.

Economic problems, 1919–23

After 1919:
- Germany's national debt was 144,000 million marks.
- By the terms of the Treaty of Versailles, Germany lost 15 per cent of its arable land, three-quarters of its iron ore and a quarter of its coal production.
- Germany had to pay enormous reparations.

The problem of inflation

Rather than reduce spending and increase taxation, Weimar governments printed more money, ensuring that inflation soared. When Germany failed to deliver reparation payments in 1923, French and Belgium troops occupied the Ruhr, Germany's industrial heartland. The value of the mark now collapsed. In December 1922 the exchange rate had been 8,000 marks to the dollar; by November 1923 it had reached 4.2 billion. By late 1923 a loaf of bread cost 100 billion marks.

Economic recovery, 1924–29

In late 1923 Germany promised to resume reparation payments and introduced a new currency – the *Rentenmark*. These measures helped end the economic crisis. Historians debate the extent of Germany's economic success between 1924 and 1929.

Economic progress?

- There was monetary stability and an influx of (mainly American) capital.
- By 1928 industrial production exceeded that of 1913.
- The Dawes Plan (1924) and the Young Plan (1929) helped Germany pay reparations.

Economic weakness?

- Unemployment remained high.
- German imports exceeded exports.
- Dependence on foreign capital made Germany susceptible to any problems in the world economic system.

The slump in agricultural prices in the 1920s

A collapse of world food prices after 1922 resulted in rural poverty. By 1929, German farmers' income was less than half the national average. Farmers made up one-third of Germany's population. Their decline in income contributed to a fall in demand within the economy as a whole.

The Great Depression

After the Wall Street Crash (1929), Americans pulled their investments from Germany – to devastating effect.
- Industrial production fell by more than 40 per cent.
- By 1932 probably 8 million Germans were unemployed.
- Those in work had their wages cuts.
- The agricultural depression deepened.

In desperation many Germans turned to the Nazis.

⊕ RAG – rate the timeline

Below are a question and a timeline. Read the question, study the timeline and, using three coloured pens, put a Red, Amber or Green star next to the issues to show:

Red: issues that have no relevance to the question

Amber: issues that have some significance to the question

Green: issues that are directly relevant to the question

How successful was the German economy in the years 1871–1933?

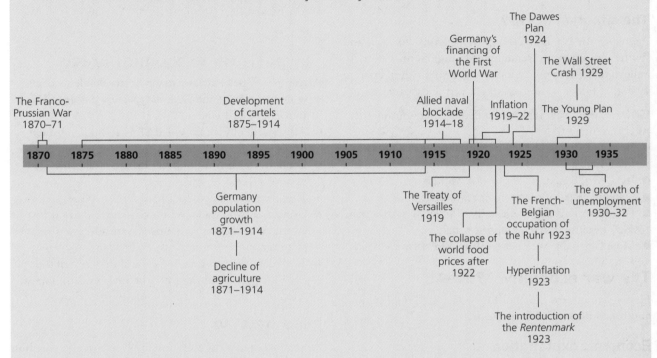

Tip: this question can be answered by including the information on page 92 with that on page 94.

ⓘ Develop the detail   ⓐ

Below are a question and the paragraph written as part of an answer to this question. The paragraph contains a limited amount of detail. Annotate the paragraph to add additional detail to the answer.

To what extent did Germany enjoy economic success in the years 1871–1933?

> After 1923 the German economy revived. Germany introduced a new currency. New reparation plans enabled Germany to pay reparations. Foreigners invested money in Germany. By 1928 industrial production levels exceeded those of 1913. But there were some problems. German agriculture, for example, did badly.

Economic change, 1933–90

The Nazi economy, 1933–39

In 1933 the Nazi government created jobs by building new roads, homes, schools and hospitals. By 1935 unemployment had fallen to 1.7 million. In 1936 Hitler launched a Four Year Plan, preparing Germany for war. As well as rearming, efforts were made to make Germany self-sufficient by developing **ersatz** products such as synthetic rubber and oil.

The situation in 1939

Arguably, the Nazis failed to provide 'guns' (for war) and 'butter' (an improved standard of living). Some historians believe that Germany's economy was so much in crisis in 1939 that Hitler was forced into a war of expansion.

However, the Nazi regime did better economically than its critics suggest.
- Between 1933 and 1936 industrial production more than doubled.
- By 1937 Germany was short of workers.
- State subsidies offered relief to farmers.
- Few historians now believe that Hitler went to war in 1939 because of the economic situation.
- Most Germans were better off in 1939 than in 1933.

The war economy, 1939–45

Having conquered much of Europe by 1941, Germany controlled huge economic resources.

Economic exploitation

Europe was organised for exploitation. Conquered countries provided food and raw materials while Germany concentrated on industrial production. Foreign workers were employed to make up for Germans serving in the armed forces. Many were appallingly treated.

Military production

Before 1941 there was little increase in German military production. The situation changed in 1941 after Germany invaded the USSR and then declared war on the USA. Between 1942 and 1944 Minister of Armaments Albert Speer succeeded in trebling German war production. But several factors limited productivity.
- Allied bombing disrupted production.
- Shortage of raw materials caused problems.
- Allied invasion in 1945 had disastrous effects.

Germany, 1945–49

Germany surrendered in May 1945. Up to 6.5 million Germans had died in the war and 20 million were homeless.

The war's legacy

- The German economy had collapsed.
- No German government remained to implement policies.
- Germans faced the prospect of starvation.
- The *Reichsmark* lost all its value. A barter economy took over.

By 1948 Germany was divided into two countries: West Germany and East Germany (under Soviet control) (see page 52).

The post-war economic miracle

After 1949 West Germany made a remarkable recovery.
- A new currency, the *Deutschmark*, was successfully introduced in 1948.
- The Marshall Plan provided $1.5 billion investment funds.
- Economics Minister Ludwig Erhard established the basis of a free economy.
- Germans initially worked hard for low wages.
- Companies and trade unions co-operated to positive effect, ensuring that grievances were addressed and that there were few strikes.
- The economy was helped by the abundance of the labour supply, resulting from the influx of millions of refugees from East Germany and Eastern Europe.

Boom, 1949–69

From 1949 to 1969 West Germany's industrial production rose threefold, faster than any other European state. Although there was a slowdown in 1965, growth was soon restored, along with full employment. Large companies, like Krupp and Siemens, dominated the German economy.

The 1970s and 1980s

The economy experienced inflationary pressures in the 1970s, largely resulting from an increase in world oil prices. Although unemployment rose, West Germany weathered the global financial storm better than its competitors.

In the 1980s growth rates improved, inflation stabilised and unemployment fell. By 1990 West Germany was the world's third-strongest industrial state and its economy was the envy of Europe. It was clearly superior to the **command economies** of the USSR and its satellites.

Simple essay style

Below is a sample question. Use your own knowledge and the information on the opposite page and page 92 to produce a plan for this question. Choose four general points and provide three pieces of specific information to support each general point. Once you have planned your essay, write the introduction and conclusion for the essay. The introduction should list the points to be discussed in the essay. The conclusion should summarise the key points and justify which point was the most important.

> How successful was economic development in Germany and West Germany in the years 1871–1990?

Spectrum of significance

Below are a question and a list of general points which could be used to answer the question. Use your own knowledge and the information on the opposite page to reach a judgement about the importance of these general points to the question posed. Write numbers on the spectrum below to indicate their relative importance. Having done this, write a brief justification of your placement, explaining why some of these factors are more important than others. The resulting diagram could form the basis of an essay plan.

> To what extent did Germany and West Germany both enjoy economic success in the years 1871–1990?

1   German industrial growth 1871–1914

2   German economic problems 1914–23

3   Economic recovery 1923–29

4   The impact of the Great Depression

5   Nazi job creation schemes 1933–36

6   Hitler's Four Year Plan (1936)

7   The German war economy 1939–45

8   The legacy of the Second World War 1945–49

9   The economic miracle 1949–70

10 The 1970s and 1980s

11 The economic situation in 1990

←——————————————————————————————————————→

Unsuccessful   **Successful**

The role of government policies in economic change, 1871–1933

Bismarck, 1871–90

Otto von Bismarck was Chancellor until 1890. For most of the 1870s, he worked with the National Liberals who supported free trade.

The introduction of protection, 1879

In 1879, Bismarck ditched free trade and the National Liberals. Aligning himself with Conservative parties, he supported the introduction of protective tariffs. He did so for several reasons.

- A slowdown in industrial growth after 1873 reduced confidence in free trade.
- France, Russia and Austria had adopted tariffs.
- German agriculture suffered from the importation of cheap wheat from the USA and Russia. Bismarck feared Germany being reliant on foreign grain.
- Tariffs would increase government revenues.
- In 1879 protectionist parties had a majority in the *Reichstag*.

While tariffs meant higher bread prices, they served to protect German jobs.

Wilhelmine Germany, 1890–1914

Wilhelm II, who became Kaiser in 1888, was determined to rule as well as reign. In 1890 he dismissed Bismarck. Wilhelm supported **Weltpolitik**. This meant expanding Germany's empire and navy.

German naval expansion

Admiral Tirpitz was given the task of expanding Germany's navy. In an effort to gain *Reichstag* support, Tirpitz was instrumental in creating the Navy League. Supported by Alfred Krupp, a great iron and steel magnate, the League soon had over 300,000 members. Pressured by the League, the *Reichstag* in 1898 and 1900 agreed to build a major fleet. Germany's naval expansion alienated Britain and led to a naval race between the two countries. Mounting naval expenditure contributed to Germany having a large budget deficit by 1914.

The First World War

Between 1914 and 1918 Germany's army leaders, claiming military necessity, interfered in all aspects of economic affairs.

Government intervention

The government tried to ensure that everyone contributed to the war effort. The War Ministry decided which men should be conscripted and which exempted. Thirteen million men were called up to serve in the armed forces – a fifth of the population. Substitute workers, especially women, helped Germany cope with its labour shortage.

The War Raw Materials Department exercised vast power – directing labour, controlling the railways, introducing rationing and price controls and allocating resources to industries. Efforts to mobilise resources increased as the war progressed. The Auxiliary Service Act (1916) enabled the government to control the labour of males between 17 and 60. Nevertheless, autocratic Germany failed to achieve the same degree of military production as democratic Britain.

Civilian morale

Lack of food and fuel made life miserable for most Germans. Workers also resented being forced to work longer hours. In November 1918, as the military and economic situation deteriorated, revolution broke out (see page 28).

The Weimar Republic, 1919–33

A series of coalition governments in the early 1920s failed to tackle Germany's financial problems. They simply printed more money. This led to increasing inflation, which reached massive proportions in 1923. While hitting many Germans (especially those with savings), **hyperinflation** freed the state of most of its debts.

Currency stabilisation

In November 1923 Stresemann's government adopted a new currency – the *Rentenmark*. This was a success and economic life revived. Weimar governments now became more fiscally responsible. They were also successful in dealing with reparation issues, agreeing to the Dawes Plan (1924) and the Young Plan (1929).

The response to the Great Depression

The Wall Street Crash (1929) led to a terrible economic crisis. As unemployment soared, governments, rather than print money as in 1923, reduced government expenditure. This led to the loss of even more jobs.

Support or challenge?

Below is a question which asks how far you agree with a specific statement. Below this is a series of general statements which are relevant to the question. Using your own knowledge and the information on the opposite page, decide whether these statements support or challenge the statement in the question and tick the appropriate box.

'Government intervention in economic matters generally benefited German economic development in the period 1871–1933.' How far do you agree with this statement?

	SUPPORT	CHALLENGE
Bismarck's support of free trade 1871–79.		
Bismarck's support for protectionism in 1879.		
Wilhelm II's support of *Weltpolitik*.		
German naval expansion 1898–1914.		
German mobilisation efforts in the First World War.		
Weimar governments' financial policies 1919–23.		
The introduction of the *Rentenmark* 1923.		
The handling of reparations 1924–29.		
Efforts to deal with the Great Depression 1930–32.		

Developing an argument

Below are a question, a list of some of the key points to be made in the essay and a paragraph from the essay. Read the question, the plan and the sample paragraph. Rewrite the paragraph in order to develop an argument. Your paragraph should explain why the factor discussed in the paragraph is either the most significant factor or less significant than another factor.

To what extent did government intervention benefit the German economy in the period 1871–1933?

Key points

- Bismarck's intervention
- Wilhelm II's intervention
- The First World War
- Weimar governments' actions 1919–23
- Weimar governments' actions 1924–33

Sample paragraph

In the First World War German military leaders interfered in economic affairs to an unprecedented degree. The German government tried to ensure that all its citizens should contribute to the war effort. The fact that some 13 million Germans were conscripted meant there was a labour shortage. The government tried to control civilian labour. It also tried to organise German economic production, no easy matter given the Allied blockade.

The role of government policies in economic change, 1933–90

Nazi economics, 1933–39

For Hitler, economics was essentially about providing the resources to achieve his racial and political goals.
- He was set on winning *Lebensraum* in eastern Europe.
- He tried to create a *Wehrwirtschaft* (defence economy).

Nazi economic policy pre-1939 was dominated by the conflicting priorities of preparing for war but also ensuring a reasonable standard of living for the German people.

The Nazi war economy

Although controlling most of Europe by 1941, the Nazis made poor use of their economic assets. Hitler initially rejected a total war effort – severe rationing, limitation of consumer goods and militarisation of civilian labour – fearing this might damage morale. Moreover, there was no unified direction of the economy. Instead there were several (often competing) organisations with power.

In 1943 Joseph Goebbels, Minister of Propaganda, called on Germans to support total war, demanding self-sacrifice to save Germany from annihilation. While war production trebled between 1942 and 1944, German productivity remained lower than that of the Allies.

Germany, 1945–49

By 1948 the US, British and French zones of Germany were merged to form West Germany.

The impact of the Marshall Plan

In 1947 US Secretary of State George Marshall announced that the USA would provide economic aid to Europe. West Germany received $1.5 billion, which greatly assisted its economic recovery.

Currency reform

In 1947–48 the Americans and British pushed ahead with plans to replace the worthless *Reichsmark* with a new currency, the *Deutschmark*. The USSR's opposition to the new currency precipitated the Berlin Blockade (1948–49). The USA and Britain supplied West Berlin by a huge airlift.

West Germany, 1949–69

After 1949, West Germany's leaders sought to create an economic system that would support a stable society.

Ludwig Erhard

Economics Minister Ludwig Erhard swept away many of the economic regulations established by the Nazis and Allies. He believed that free market forces would ensure prosperity. He also tried to ensure a 'social market', whereby the government provided generous welfare benefits for the more vulnerable in society.

The Stabilisation Law

In 1967 Karl Schiller, the new Economics Minister, supported the Stabilisation Law. This gave the West German government greater authority to direct the economy in times of recession.

The impact of membership of the European Community

European economic integration began in 1951 when trade restrictions on coal and steel were dropped between Belgium, France, Italy, Luxembourg, the Netherlands and West Germany (the 'six'). Integration took a big step forward as a result of the Treaty of Rome (1957) by which the 'six' formed the European Economic Community (EEC). The main economic benefits to West Germany of closer European integration were:
- cheaper products through the elimination of trade barriers
- savings achieved through common policies of agriculture and transport
- easier flow of skilled labour around the EEC.

German leaders also supported:
- monetary union (the adoption of a common European currency)
- political union (creating of a single European state).

Little progress towards these goals was achieved pre-1990.

The Common Agricultural Policy

The Common Agricultural Policy (CAP) was established in 1962. CAP ensured that agricultural policies were harmonious and transferred to European Community level. Essentially CAP was a compromise between West Germany and France. West German industry would have access to the French market. In exchange West Germany would help pay French farmers.

Western co-operation

In the 1970s Chancellor Schmidt promoted Western co-operation in tackling common economic problems.
- He helped establish regular meetings between the most important economic nations.
- He was instrumental in creating the European Exchange Rate Mechanism (ERM) to promote monetary stability.

The impact of Chancellor Kohl

In an effort to reduce the state's role in the economy, Kohl's government carried through a series of privatisation measures, selling shares of several state-owned institutions such as Volkswagen and Lufthansa.

Mind map

Use the information on the opposite page to add detail to the mind map below. This should assist your understanding of the impact of government intervention on German economic development.

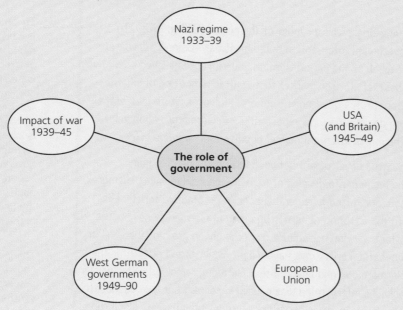

 Complete the paragraph   a

Below are a question and a paragraph written as part of an answer to the question. The paragraph contains a point and specific examples, but lacks a concluding explanatory link back to the question. Complete the paragraph, adding this link in the space provided.

How successful was government intervention in the economic development of Germany and West Germany in the years 1871–90?

Between 1945 and 1949 Germany was divided into four zones and governed by the USA, Britain, France and the Soviet Union. The USA, in particular, soon aimed to restore the German economy, hoping that West Germany would then be a major ally against Communist expansion. In 1947 the US Secretary of State George Marshall offered economic aid to Europe. West Germany ultimately received nearly $1.5 billion in aid. The USA (and Britain) also helped Germany establish a new currency — the *Deutschmark*.

_____

_____

Exam focus

Below is a high level essay. Read it and the comments around it.

To what extent did government intervention affect the development of the German economy in the years 1871–1990?

The German economy performed amazingly well for most of the period 1871 to 1990. To a certain extent this was due to government intervention and, somewhat ironically, deliberate government non-intervention. For much of the period German governments believed essentially that economic development was best left to free market forces. (It is a moot point whether non-government action actually constitutes government action!) However, at various stages German governments did intervene decisively – and importantly – in Germany's economic development. As this essay will show, this intervention had positive and negative effects.

> The introduction is well focused. It deals with many of the crucial issues, comments shrewdly on whether lack of intervention is actually an important government action, and gives a good indication of the likely course of the essay.

Given the success of German industrial development between 1871 and 1914, German governments generally allowed the economy to develop of its own accord. However, Bismarck intervened decisively in 1879, abandoning free trade and supporting protective tariffs. His actions were partly in response to the adoption of tariffs by many of Germany's neighbours. His measures, largely designed to protect German agriculture from the cheap grain of the USA and Russia, were perceived to be successful. Tariffs may have meant higher bread prices for the people but they probably saved German jobs and ensured that Germany remained self-sufficient in terms of food production. Wilhelm II's intervention was equally important but less successful. His policy of *Weltpolitik* and naval expansion, while benefiting German industrialists like Krupp, led to budget deficits and rivalry with Britain – which was of crucial importance in 1914.

> This paragraph shows impressive powers of synthesis. It also shows detailed knowledge of the economic situation in Germany pre-1914.

German governments, dominated by military leaders, intervened in all aspects of economic affairs during the First World War. German rulers tried to ensure that all the country's citizens contributed to the war effort. The War Ministry decided which men should be conscripted and which exempted. Faced with the consequences of the Allied naval blockade, the War Raw Materials Department exercised vast power – directing labour, controlling the railways, introducing rationing and price controls and allocating resources to industries competing for scarce raw material. Government efforts to mobilise German resources more thoroughly increased in 1916–17. The Auxiliary Serve Act enabled the government to control the labour of all males aged between 17 and 60 while a Supreme War Office was given wide powers over industry. Despite such measures, Germany lost the First World War. Somewhat ironically, autocratic Germany failed to achieve the same degree of economic mobilisation as democratic Britain.

> This paragraph deals succinctly with German governments' efforts to mobilise economic resources between 1914 and 1918. The last sentence is powerful although it begs the question why Germany was less successful than Britain.

The spate of Weimar coalition governments between 1919 and 1933 restored economic freedom. Their main impact on economic life was in the realm of finance. Between 1919 and 1923 Weimar governments made no attempt to balance the budget and simply issued vast quantities of paper money. While this may have prevented unemployment, it eventually led to the hyperinflation of 1923. This followed the French–Belgian occupation of the Ruhr when Germany failed to meet its reparation obligations. Stresemann's government managed to prevent a complete economic meltdown, introducing a new currency (the *Rentenmark*) and agreeing to pay reparations. Thereafter Weimar governments were more fiscally prudent. This policy backfired, however, with the onset of the Great Depression following the Wall Street Crash. As millions of Germans lost their jobs, Weimar governments were determined to balance the budget, cutting expenditure and making even more Germans redundant. Lack of government intervention and perceived Weimar economic failure encouraged the rise of the Nazis.

> This paragraph demonstrates an excellent understanding of the Weimar economic situation. It again raises the issue of when lack of action is in fact action!

Hitler's government intervened decisively in economic matters. Government work creation schemes, supervised by Schacht, succeeded in getting Germans back to work. Nazi policies were so successful that by 1937 Germany was actually short of workers. Hitler's Four Year Plan – his efforts to prepare Germany for war – were less successful. While the German economy was able to produce both 'guns' and 'butter', Hitler's desire to expand German territory ultimately brought about the Second World War. Nazi efforts to run a war economy were initially shambolic. Between 1939 and 1941 various government agencies were in competition and Hitler made little attempt to put Germany on a total war-footing. The situation changed in 1942 when Speer became Minister of Armaments. War production trebled between 1942 and 1944, partly because of the appalling exploitation of foreign/slave labour. However, Speer's efforts and Goebbels' calls for total war failed to produce a German miracle. By 1945 Germany was totally crushed and its economy in ruins.

> This paragraph again shows an ability to cut to the chase, focusing on key developments.

The intervention of the American government helped create West Germany and restore its economy. In 1947 Secretary of State George Marshall offered European countries large sums of American money. West Germany seized the opportunity and was given $1.5 billion, money which helped to kick-start its economy. The Americans, with British help, also helped introduce a new German currency – the *Deutschmark*. This was launched successfully in 1948 and was a vital foundation of the West Germany economy.

> The candidate shows that non-German government intervention greatly assisted the West German economy after 1945.

The West German economic miracle after 1949 – industrial production trebled between 1950 and 1960 – was in part due to the policies of Economics Minister Ludwig Erhard. Erhard favoured free markets. However, he – and his successors – also supported welfare measures which provided support for the most vulnerable in society. West Germany thus evolved into a successful welfare state. In the 1950s the West Germany government also embraced European economic integration. The Treaty of Rome (1957) established the European Economic Community – a common or single economic market for all those who belonged to it. For German ministers, from Adenauer onwards, economic integration was seen as a step towards longer-term goals: monetary and political union. These goals were not realised. But by 1990 West Germany's economy, which under Chancellor Kohl supported more free enterprise, was the strongest in Europe.

> A good paragraph which brings the chronological synthesis to a compelling end. It provides evidence that the candidate's knowledge of the West German economic situation and government policy is first rate.

Thus, government intervention played a crucial role, both in Germany's economic development and in the development of the West Germany economy. Intervention was not always for 'good'. Nazi economic intervention, albeit initially successful, was designed to support expansion and war. This ultimately brought about disaster. West Germany was assisted by Allied (largely US) government action in the late 1940s. But after 1949 it again stood on its own feet, its governments, left and right, supporting capitalist free enterprise, bolstered by a raft of welfare measures to assist society's losers. By 1990 it was clear that the West Germany example of – light – government intervention was far more successful than the socialist 'command' economy of East Germany. This was an important factor in German reunification in 1990.

> The conclusion pulls together the argument that was initiated in the introduction and developed throughout the essay.

This is a Level 5 essay. It demonstrates detailed knowledge of a range of different issues. It also clearly engages with the question, offering a balanced and carefully reasoned argument which is sustained throughout the essay.

What makes a good answer?

Use this essay and the comments to make a bullet-pointed list of the characteristics of a Level 5 answer. Use this list when planning and writing your own practice exam essays.

Glossary

Allied powers   The main opponents of Germany in the Second World War – Britain, France, the USA and the USSR.

Allies   The main opponents of Germany in the First World War – Britain, France, Russia (pre-1918) and the USA (from 1917).

Anarchist   A person whose ideal society is one without government of any kind. Late nineteenth-century anarchists often sought to bring about such a condition by terrorism.

Armistice   An agreement to stop fighting at the end of a war.

Artisan   A skilled manual worker.

Autocracy   A government ruled essentially by one person.

Bourgeoisie   The middle class – doctors, lawyers, teachers, civil servants, businessmen, clergymen.

Cartel   An association of manufacturers who come to a contractual agreement about the level of production and the scale of prices and maintain a monopoly.

Command economy   The system by which the state organises all aspects of the economy.

Concentration camps   These were places where political opponents of the Nazis were imprisoned after 1933. In the Second World War, many concentration camps were used to exterminate Jews and other perceived enemies of the Third Reich.

Concordat   A pact or agreement, often between the Pope and the government of a nation.

Doppelverdienerinnen   This translates as 'second-wage earner'. It was a term of abuse aimed at married women who went out to work.

Ersatz   An artificial substitute for something natural.

Federal   A political system where substantial power is held at regional level over aspects of government such as education and policing.

Franchise   The right to vote.

Free trade   Unrestricted trade without protective import duties.

Freikorps   Voluntary soldiers, most of whom had fought in the First World War, who were strongly nationalistic and anti-socialist.

Functionalist (or structuralist)   These are terms used to describe historians who believe that Hitler did not have as much control over events as 'intentionalist' historians believe.

Gauleiter   A Nazi Party leader who was head of a regional area (or *Gau*).

Gleichschaltung   The word translates as 'co-ordination'. Hitler's consolidation of power (1933–34) is often referred to as *Gleichschaltung*.

Great Depression   This world-wide economic downturn followed the Wall Street Crash in the USA in 1929. The Depression led to increasing unemployment in the USA and Europe, particularly in Germany.

Gross national product   The total value of all goods and services produced within a country.

Hyperinflation   This happens when the amount of money in an economy increases massively. This pushes prices up and the spiral of printing money spins out of control.

Holocaust   The mass murder of Jews and other groups (e.g. physically and mentally handicapped people, Gypsies, Soviet prisoners of war), undertaken by Hitler's government during the Second World War.

Inflation   This results from governments issuing too much paper money, leading to a decline in a currency's purchasing power.

Intentionalist   Term used to describe scholars who believe that Hitler was fully in control in the Third Reich and able to get his way on most issues.

Jesuits   A Catholic order of priests whose members supported papal authority.

Kulturkampf   This translates as 'struggle for culture' or 'struggle for civilisation'. In Germany, after 1871 the struggle was essentially between the state and the Catholic Church.

Lebensraum   This translates as 'living space'. Hitler planned to win territory in the east on which 'superior' Germans would settle, evicting 'inferior' Slavs.

Marshall Plan   The plan undertaken by US Secretary of State George Marshall in 1948 to provide huge economic aid to Europe.

Nationalisation   Government ownership.

NATO   This stands for the North Atlantic Treaty Organisation. This was an alliance, created in 1949, to protect the Western world against possible Soviet aggression. Its original members were Belgium, Canada, Denmark, France, Iceland, Italy, Luxembourg, the Netherlands, Norway, Portugal, the UK and the USA. Greece and Turkey joined in 1952, West Germany in 1955. The organisation remains important to this day.

Nuremberg rally   Since 1927 the Nazi Party held its main political meeting in the German town of Nuremberg. The rallies attracted tens of thousands of Nazi members. They gave the impression of strength and unity.

Papal infallibility   The idea that papal pronouncements on matters of faith and morals should not be questioned.

Plebiscite   A vote on a single issue on which the whole electorate is asked a yes/no question; an old-fashioned term for a referendum.

Politburo   The policy-making committee (and thus effectively the government) in East European Communist states.

Proletariat   A term used to describe the poorest working classes who laboured in factories, mills and mines.

Proportional representation   This system of voting ensures that a party receives the same percentage of seats as of votes received.

Putsch   An attempted overthrow of a government by the use of force.

Realpolitik   The term used to describe the ruthless and cynical policies of politicians; for example, Bismarck's, whose main aim was to increase the power of the Prussian and later the German state by whatever means were available to him.

Reichsbank   A national German bank, similar to the Bank of England.

Revolutionary shop stewards   These were working-class activists who tried to organise mass action in the factories to end the war.

SA (*Sturm-Abteilung*)   The paramilitary wing of the Nazi Party. Its members (storm-troopers) wore brown-shirts. Their task was to protect Nazi meetings and break up meetings of Nazi enemies. By the early 1930s hundreds of thousands of Germans belonged to the SA.

Satellite state   A country essentially under the control of a more powerful country.

Secede   To leave or quit.

Secular   Non-religious.

Sovereignty   Ultimate power.

Soviet   Soviets were councils of workers, peasants and soldiers. Such councils had been created in Russia in 1917, eventually allowing the Bolsheviks to come to power.

SS (*Schutzstaffel*)   This organisation began as Hitler's personal bodyguard. Led by Heinrich Himmler, the SS after 1933 became the main agents of terror in Nazi Germany. Members were fiercely loyal to Hitler and his ideas.

Third Reich   This was the name Hitler gave to his Nazi regime. The first Reich had existed in the Middle Ages. The second was that from 1871-1918. Hitler boasted that his Third Reich would last a thousand years.

Totalitarian   A form of government that controls everything and allows no opposition.

Truman Doctrine   President Truman's pronouncement (in 1947) that the USA would give economic and military aid to those countries threatened by Communist take-over.

USSR   The Union of Soviet Socialist Republics – formerly the Russian Empire; it was formed in 1922.

Veto   The power or right to reject or forbid a proposed measure.

War credits   Financial bills passed by the *Reichstag* to enable the German government to fund the First World War.

Weimar Republic   This is the name usually given to Germany between 1919 and 1933.

Weltpolitik   This translates as 'world policy'. The term is used to describe Wilhelm II's world power ambitions.

Key figures

Konrad Adenauer (1876–1967)   Adenauer, a devout Roman Catholic and first leader of the Christian Democratic Union, became first post-war Chancellor of West Germany in 1949. He remained in power until 1963, leading his country from the ruins of the Second World War to become a productive, prosperous and stable nation.

Otto von Bismarck (1815–98)   Bismarck came to power in Prussia in 1862. His policies led to three wars against Denmark, Austria and France and resulted in the establishment of the second German Empire in 1871. He became first Chancellor of the *Kaiserreich*, serving until 1890. Known as the Iron Chancellor, he was opposed to socialism. He also came into conflict with the Roman Catholic Church. A brilliant diplomat, he helped maintain peace in Europe after 1871.

Willy Brandt (1913–92)   Brandt, a socialist, fled to Norway and then Sweden during the Third Reich. A leading member of the SPD, he became Mayor of West Berlin (1957–66), leader of the SPD (1964–87) and Chancellor of West Germany (1969–74).

George Bush (born 1924)   George Bush was Vice-President of the USA from 1981–89. In 1989 he became the 41st President, serving until 1993. His presidency was mainly concerned with foreign affairs, not least the ending of the Cold War. His son, also called George, became the 43rd President (2001–09).

Friedrich Ebert (1871–1925)   Ebert, leader of the SPD, became the leader of Germany in November 1918 after Kaiser Wilhelm's abdication. He was elected the first President of the Weimar Republic in 1919 and served until his death.

Joseph Goebbels (1897–1945)   Goebbels was the influential Minister of Propaganda in Nazi Germany from 1933 to 1945. He committed suicide in Hitler's bunker in May 1945.

Mikhail Gorbachev (born 1931)   Gorbachev was General Secretary of the Communist Party of the Soviet Union and last leader of the USSR from 1985 until 1991. He supported liberal policies of *glasnost* (openness) and *perestroika* (restructuring) and his policies contributed to the unification of Germany and the end of the Cold War.

Heinrich Himmler (1900–45)   Himmler was leader of the dreaded SS. A fanatical Nazi, he was deeply involved in the Holocaust. He committed suicide in May 1945.

Field Marshal Paul von Hindenburg (1847–1934)   Hindenburg was one of Germany's most respected leaders in the First World War. A conservative nationalist, he served as second President of the Weimar Republic, appointing Hitler as Chancellor in January 1933.

Adolf Hitler (1889–1945)   Hitler, probably the most famous 'German' of the twentieth century, was actually born in Austria. After the First World War, he became leader of the Nazi Party. The failure of the Munich Putsch in 1923 did not end his political career. In 1933 he became Chancellor of Germany and he was Führer of Nazi Germany from 1933 to 1945. In 1939 he led Germany into the Second World War and was hugely responsible for the Holocaust. He committed suicide in Berlin in 1945.

Erich Honecker (1912–94)   Honecker, a Communist, was imprisoned during the Third Reich. After 1945 he rose to power in East Germany, becoming General Secretary of the SED in 1971 and effective leader of East Germany until 1989.

Helmut Kohl (born 1930)   Kohl served as chairman of the CDU from 1973 to 1998. He was Chancellor of West Germany from 1982 to 1990 and Chancellor of the reunited Germany from 1990 to 1998. His sixteen-year tenure was the longest of any German Chancellor since Bismarck. He is widely regarded as the main architect of German reunification and of the Maastricht Treaty which established the European Union.

Rosa Luxemburg (1871–1919)   Rosa Luxemburg was a Marxist theorist and activist of Polish-Jewish descent who became a naturalised German citizen. In 1915 she co-founded the anti-war Spartacus League (with Karl Liebknecht). She was murdered (with Liebknecht) in Berlin in 1919 during the Spartacist uprising.

Kurt Schumacher (1895–1952)   Schumacher, a Social Democrat, spent over ten years in Nazi concentration camps where he was severely mistreated. He became chairman of the SPD in 1946 and the first Leader of the Opposition in West Germany from 1949 to 1952. He strongly opposed both Adenauer and East German communism.

Timeline

1871	Prussia's victory in the Franco-Prussian War led to German unification		Death of Hindenburg: Hitler became both President and Chancellor
1872	Start of the *Kulturkampf*		Schacht's New Plan
1878–79	The end of the *Kulturkampf*	**1935**	Nuremberg Laws passed
1879	Bismarck introduced protective tariffs and split with the National Liberals	**1938**	Union with Austria
1888	Wilhelm II became Kaiser		Take-over of Sudetenland
1890	Bismarck was forced to resign	**1939**	Germany invaded Poland: start of the Second World War
1897	Germany began to pursue *Weltpolitik*	**1940**	Hitler conquered most of western Europe
1914	Start of the First World War	**1941**	German invasion of the USSR
1916	Establishment of the 'silent dictatorship' of Hindenburg and Ludendorff		Systematic massacre of Jews in the USSR
1918	Outbreak of revolution in Germany	**1942**	Wannsee Conference
	Abdication of Kaiser Wilhelm II		Speer appointed Minister of Munitions
	Armistice	**1945**	Hitler committed suicide
1919	Spartacist uprising		End of Second World War
	National Assembly elections		Germany (and Berlin) divided into four occupation zones
	Ebert elected President		Nuremberg Trials
	Weimar constitution adopted	**1947**	The Bizone was formed
	Treaty of Versailles signed		Announcement of the Truman Doctrine
1923	French and Belgium troops occupied the Ruhr		Announcement of the Marshall Plan
	Hyperinflation crisis	**1948**	The *Deutschmark* was introduced into the Western zones of Germany
1924	Dawes Plan	**1948–49**	Soviet blockade of Berlin: Allied air lift
1929	Young Plan	**1949**	Establishment of the FRG
	Wall Street Crash		Adenauer became West German Chancellor
1932	The Nazis became the largest party in the *Reichstag*		Establishment of the GDR
1933	Hitler appointed Chancellor	**1957**	The Treaty of Rome
	Reichstag Fire	**1961**	Building of the Berlin Wall
	(March) election: Nazis and Nationalists won an overall majority	**1963**	Adenauer resigned
	Enabling Act	**1982**	Kohl became Chancellor of a CDU/FDP coalition
	All political parties, except for the Nazis disbanded	**1989**	Revolution from below in East Germany
	Trade unions disbanded		Fall of the Berlin Wall
	Concordat agreed between the Nazis and the Roman Catholic Church	**1990**	Free East German elections
1934	Night of the Long Knives		The Currency Union
			German reunification

Answers

Key Topic 1 Ruling the Second Reich, 1871–79

Page 7, Complete the paragraph

The role of the Emperor within the constitution of the Second Reich suggests that the constitution was fundamentally undemocratic. For example, **under the 1871 constitution, the Kaiser, without reference to the German people, could appoint and dismiss the Chancellor and other government ministers. He could also dissolve the *Reichstag*. As well as being President of the *Bundesrat*, the Kaiser was Commander-in-Chief of Germany's armed forces. German officers and men swore an oath of allegiance to the Kaiser, not to the government. Thus, the army was accountable to the Kaiser and could not be controlled by the democratically elected *Reichstag*.** Accordingly, the Emperor's role suggests that the Second Reich's constitution was fundamentally undemocratic because ultimately the Emperor had considerable power and was unaccountable to the German people.

Page 7, Eliminate irrelevance

The *Reichstag*, or Parliament, was clearly the most democratic element of the Second Reich's constitution. ~~The constitution was devised by Bismarck following Prussia's – or perhaps Germany's – victory over France in 1870–71. It very much mirrored the North German Confederation, also drawn up by Bismarck, following Prussia's victory over Austria in 1866. The 1867 constitution had to be redrawn because four more states had now joined what had become the Second Reich.~~ Bismarck, a Prussian landowner, did not have much sympathy with democracy. Nevertheless, he realised that it would be foolish to deny the German people a say in the way Germany was governed. The *Reichstag* ensured the people had a voice. It was elected by all men over the age of 25 and was thus far more representative than most parliaments, including Britain's, at this time. It had the power to reject, accept and amend any law. It should be said that there were limits to the power of the *Reichstag*. It could not introduce new laws. Nor could it elect – or eject – the Chancellor. Nevertheless, the *Reichstag* is evidence that there was a strong democratic element within the Second Reich's constitution.

Page 9, Spot the mistake

The paragraph does not get into Level 4 because, although the examples are focused on the question, they lack specific detail.

Page 9, Develop the detail

To a large extent Prussia did control Germany in the 1870s. William the Prussian King, became German Emperor. **As such, he was head of the imperial executive and supreme warlord of the Reich's armed forces.** Bismarck, the Prussian Prime Minister, became German Chancellor. **Except for the period 1872–73, he held both offices simultaneously.** Prussia, the biggest state, **with 60 per cent of Germany's population and two-thirds of its territory,** dominated both the *Reichstag* and the *Bundesrat*. **Prussia returned 235 deputies out of a total of 397 in the *Reichstag*. The fact that it had 17 seats in the *Bundesrat* meant it could block any unwelcome constitutional amendments.** Prussian aristocrats had considerable power over the German government, German administration and the German army.

Key Topic 2 The birth of democratic Germany, 1917–19

Page 23, Develop the detail

By 1917 Germany faced major economic problems. Germany was short of food **and by 1917 virtually every foodstuff was rationed. To make matters worse, over the winter of 1916–17 Germany suffered serious shortages of coal and transport. Civilian deaths from starvation and hypothermia were increasing rapidly.** Life for most Germans was truly miserable. This meant that there was growing discontent among civilians. **Many workers resented being forced to work even longer hours as a result of the Auxiliary Service Act. Considerable anger was also harboured against industrialists who were making vast profits from the war. Trade unions organised an increasing number of strikes.** In many ways Germany's internal problems were as serious as its military problems.

Page 27, Complete the paragraph

In early November the revolutionary situation in Germany gathered momentum. On 7 November Majority Socialist leaders threatened to withdraw support from the government unless Wilhelm abdicated and socialists were given greater representation in the cabinet. When Prince Max failed to persuade Wilhelm to abdicate, the Majority Socialist ministers Scheidemann and Bauer resigned. The Majority Socialists now agreed to support a general strike on 9 November. By 9 November virtually all Germany's army leaders realised that the Kaiser had to go. Abandoned by his generals, Wilhelm accepted the reality of the situation and fled to the Netherlands. Prince Max resigned and a new government, led by the Majority Socialist leader Ebert, came to power. **The abdication of the Kaiser and the coming to power of a socialist government were revolutionary events in their own right. By early November 1918 it seemed to many that Germany was on the brink of an even greater Russian-style revolution.**

Page 31, Spot the mistake

The paragraph does not get into Level 4 because although the examples are relevant to the question, they lack specific detail. Nor is there an explanatory link at the end of the paragraph, linking the examples back to the question.

Page 31, Develop the detail

Following elections **on 19 January 1919**, a National Assembly met in Weimar to agree to a new constitution. **The election results were a triumph for the forces of parliamentary democracy. Over 80 per cent of the electorate (including women for the first time) turned out to vote.** The largest party in the Assembly was the SPD, **which won 165 seats (38 per cent of the vote). On 10 February 1919** SPD leader Ebert was elected as **first** President **of the new Republic**. But this was not a total triumph for Ebert. Lacking an overall majority, the SPD had to co-operate with other pro-democracy parties. **The SPD found allies in the Centre and Democrat parties. Over 75 per cent of the electorate had voted for the SPD, Centre and Democrat parties, all of which were committed to the new Republic. The new government was headed by Scheidemann and consisted of six Social Democrats, three Centrists and three Democrats. The election results thus seemed a triumph for Ebert and his party.**

Key Topic 3 A new Reich, 1933–35

Page 37, Complete the paragraph

In March 1933 the *Reichstag* passed the Enabling Act. It appeared to be legal. **In reality, the passing of the Act was the result of political calculation and corruption masquerading as legitimacy. To change the constitution, Hitler needed a two-thirds majority. He obtained this by preventing the 81 Communist members taking their seats in the Reichstag and imprisoning 26 SPD deputies. The Nationalists readily gave Hitler their support. So did the Centre Party in return for an assurance that the Nazis would allow the Catholic Church absolute independence in Germany. The Enabling Act, which gave Hitler the right to rule by decree for four years, passed by 441 votes to 94 on 24 March. Hitler's government could now pass laws**

without consulting the Reichstag. The passing of the Enabling Act ensured that by the end of March 1933 Germany was well on the way to being a one-party Nazi state.

Page 39, Write the question

Assess the value of the source for revealing **Hitler's role in the events of 30 June 1934** and in **the efficiency of the Nazi regime.** Explain your answer, using the source, the information given about its origin and your own knowledge about the historical context.

Page 41, Complete the paragraph

Immediately after the end of the Second World War, the image of the Nazi state was one that was hierarchically organised, with all power concentrated in Hitler's hands. **The truth was rather different. The Nazi state was far from a smooth-functioning, rationally organised regime. Indeed, there was no coherent system of government in the Third Reich. Party bureaucracies expanded, operating in parallel with existing state ministries. The lines of power and authority between state and party blurred amidst a struggle for influence. In consequence, it is often hard to know who was making decisions in Nazi Germany. Nazi propaganda declared that Hitler was at the centre of things, responsible for all major decision-making. But he was rarely involved in the day-to-day discussions which led to the formulation of policy. Cabinet meetings were infrequent and he did not see some ministers for months at a time. His preference for his home in Bavaria instead of Berlin and his aversion to systematic work meant that decision-making was often a chaotic process. It is even possible to claim that the anarchic system controlled Hitler rather than he the system.** Thus, in reality, because of the nature of the Nazi state and his own character, Hitler was rather a weak dictator.

Page 45, Develop the detail

Nazi propaganda did much to persuade Germans that Nazi rule was a 'good thing'. Germans in the Third Reich were given just one view of the situation: the Nazi view. Joseph Goebbels, **Minister of Popular Enlightenment and Propaganda from 1933**, was crucial to this whole process. **His ministry was responsible for the control of books, the press, radio and films. Realising the importance of radio as a medium for propaganda, Goebbels encouraged the mass production of cheap radios. Painting, sculpture and architecture were also brought under Nazi control. Goebbels encouraged all Germans to identify with the Third Reich. (The 'Heil Hitler' greeting, for example, was intended to strengthen identification with the regime.)** Nazi indoctrination of youth was another feature of the way the Nazi regime tried to ensure that Germans, particularly the next generation of Germans, would support Nazi ideology. **By 1935 it was virtually compulsory to belong to one of the Hitler Youth Movements. The aim of these movements was to ensure that young Germans were loyal to fatherland and Führer. Meanwhile, ideologically unreliable teachers were dismissed, racial education became compulsory and subjects like history were used as a vehicle for Nazi ideas.** Nazi propaganda and indoctrination undoubtedly helped convince many Germans that Hitler was some kind of 'superman'.

Key Topic 4 Establishing and ruling the new Federal Republic, 1949–60

Page 53, Develop the detail

In 1945 Germany was divided into four zones of occupation – British, French, American and Russian. **Britain was to occupy north-western Germany, the USA the south, France the south-west and the USSR the east. Berlin too was divided into four occupation sectors.** The four powers acted jointly through the Allied Control Council, **which comprised the military commanders of the four Allied nations.** But generally each of the Allies ran their zones more or less independently. **The original intention was to treat Germany as one economic unit, that it would remain united, and that it would be neutral and disarmed. However, the Allies had no clear or agreed vision of what the new Germany should look like or how it should be governed. As the Cold War developed after 1945, the prospect of a united Germany became more and more unlikely. The USA and Britain soon merged their zones into the so-called Bizone, which the French zone belatedly joined in 1948.** By 1948 the Soviet zone was clearly separate from the Western zones.

Page 55, Complete the paragraph

The Federal Parliament under the Basic Law was not dissimilar to the Weimar constitution. **As in the Weimar constitution, there were to be two chambers, or houses, of parliament. One house, the *Bundestag*, was to be elected every four years through universal suffrage. The other, the *Bundesrat*, was made up of representatives of each state, or *Land*. However, there were important differences. Although Germany still had a system of proportional representation, crucially, political parties now needed to win over five per cent of the vote to gain representation in the *Bundestag*. This was intended to prevent too many parties, which had led to political fragmentation and short-lived governments between 1919 and 1933.**

Moreover, any political parties which opposed the constitution could be banned. The aim was to prevent Nazi or Communist parties participating in the political process, as in the Weimar period, with the intent of using democratic means to destroy democracy. Thus, the Basic Law, learning the lessons of the Weimar constitution, tried to ensure that West Germany would have political stability.

Page 55, Eliminate irrelevance

The Presidents of West Germany had very different powers to those given to the Presidents of the Weimar Republic. Weimar Presidents had been elected by popular vote every seven years. They also held substantial powers, such as those specified in Article 48, which allowed Presidents to rule by decree in times of emergency or government instability. This had been a major problem in Germany, especially in the period 1930–33. ~~In the economic and political crisis following the Wall Street Crash in America in 1929, President Hindenburg had largely ignored the *Reichstag* and appointed Chancellors he thought were suitable men to run the country. In the end he had appointed Adolf Hitler as Chancellor of Germany on 30 January 1933, even though Hitler did not command a majority in the *Reichstag*.~~ Under the Basic Law, by contrast, Presidents had relatively few powers. Elected by *Bundestag* members and representatives of each *Land* parliament, they were largely ceremonial heads of state. They had no power to rule by decree or appoint Chancellors at whim. Lessons had clearly been learned by the Basic Law founders.

Page 57, Write the question

Assess the value of Source 1 for **revealing the situation in Germany in 1949 and Adenauer's intentions on becoming Chancellor in 1949.** Explain your answer, using the source, the information given about its origin and your own knowledge about the historical context.

Page 63, Complete the paragraph

There is no doubt that throughout the period 1949–60 West Germans were committed to democracy. In 1949 the Western Allies wondered whether the FRG could provide a stable democracy. Many feared that Weimar conditions would re-surface, resulting in the reappearance of authoritarian government and possibly a revival of Nazism. Neither the political fragmentation nor the revival occurred. The safeguards built into the constitution, particularly the five per cent rule, contributed to the FRG's stability. So did West Germany's economic success. This was vital in ensuring support for democracy, contrary to the way in which economic depression had led many Germans to abandon Weimar democracy. Nor is there any doubt that Chancellor Adenauer was committed to democracy. **Nevertheless, this did not necessarily mean that all West Germans had abandoned Nazism and all it stood for.**

Key Topic 5 Reunification: recreating a united Germany, 1989–90

Page 69, Develop the detail

In late September and early October, there were signs of growing unrest in East German cities. **The Civic Revolution in the GDR – its so-called 'democratic awakening' – suggests that the SED's refusal to tolerate loyal criticism meant that its critics had little alternative but to pursue a 'revolution from below'.** Leipzig, one of the main centres of opposition, had a number of Monday demonstrations, which grew in size each week. **On 25 September some 10,000 people took part. By 9 October a crowd estimated at 70,000 assembled to call for peaceful dialogue. East German leader Honecker wanted to crush the demonstrators. But he found himself at odds with Egon Krenz, deputy chairman of the council of state, who had the backing of the Soviet Ambassador in East Berlin.** By mid-October it was clear that Honecker was in danger of losing control.

Page 75, Complete the paragraph

The Two Plus Four Treaty was vital. Germany could not be unified until the four victorious Allied powers of 1945 accepted the fact. The USSR was the nation most likely to oppose unification. But Mikhail Gorbachev, the Soviet leader, by mid-1990 accepted the necessity of unification. He struck a hard bargain for his support. Chancellor Kohl had to agree to domestic troop reductions, to provide considerable financial and technical aid to the USSR and pay for the removal of Soviet troops from former GDR territory. Thus, in September 1990 the Two Plus Four Treaty was agreed. The four Allied powers renounced all their rights in Germany while the still two Germanies confirmed the 1945 borders and renounced any future territorial claims beyond those existing borders. **Certainly Germany was well on the way to union before the Two Plus Four Treaty. But once it was agreed, the final obstacle to unification was cleared. In that sense, it was the most important of all the treaties agreed in 1990.**

Page 77, Develop the detail

One of the economic problems was the cost of unification. This mainly fell on what had been West Germany. **Kohl's government pretended that the costs could be financed by a balanced growth in the economy but they were deliberately deceiving the electorate in the West.** The West Germans took over East Germany's huge debts, **which were estimated to be in excess of 600,000 million marks. In addition it was ready to underwrite the risks of the newly created Public Trust which had responsibility for the privatisation of state holdings** and the return of private property to its lawful owners. This proved a costly business. When it finally wound up its affairs it was 256 billion marks in the red. The West Germans also had to support East Germany's antiquated economy and pay for its social services. **Many East German enterprises were unable to compete with those of the West and had to be closed down. As unemployment in East Germany rose, so did West German loans to the East.** The costs were astronomic.

Theme 1 Social change in Germany and West Germany, 1871–1990

Page 83, Complete the paragraph

In 1871 most Germans lived and worked on the land. By 1914, however, the situation had changed. **The flight from the countryside to the towns built up speed after 1880. Industrial employment seemed attractive to rural workers. Whereas peasants laboured for long hours for little pay, between 1885 and 1913 the wages of industrial workers rose and working hours fell by a third. While there were still some 7 million agricultural workers in 1914, many felt they were outcasts, disadvantaged with regard to pay, education provision and medical care. By 1900 a rural child was more likely to die before the age of one than an urban one. Compared with the modernity of urban life, the countryside seemed more backward. Given Germany's growing industrial economy, job opportunities in the cities continued to increase and the exodus from the land continued to accelerate.** Thus, by 1914 most Germans belonged to the urban working class – the proletariat. This was the main social development in the period from 1871 to 1914.

Page 85, Develop the detail

One of Hitler's aims in 1933 was to create a 'people's community', uniting all ethnic Germans. He also hoped to promote social mobility. Some progress was made towards achieving this goal. **The Nazis encouraged the acquisition of new skills in the workforce, greatly expanded vocational training programmes, and offered generous incentives for advancement of 'efficient' workers. Both National Socialist ideology and Hitler's basic outlook inclined the regime to favour breaking down class differences. Hitler was fully conscious that the working class had traditional left-wing leanings. Determined not to risk alienating the proletariat, he supported the creation of the German Labour Front, which did much to improve working conditions in factories.** More might have been done but for the outbreak of the Second World War.

Page 87, Spot the mistake

The paragraph does not get into Level 4 because although the examples are relevant to the question, they lack specific detail. Nor is there an explanatory link at the end of the paragraph, linking the examples back to the question.

Page 89, Eliminate irrelevance

The Third Reich did little to encourage equal rights for women. Hitler and the Nazis were profoundly anti-feminist. They believed that women should be confined to their 'natural' roles as wives and mothers. Hitler, in particular, stressed the importance of *Kinder, Kirche, Küche* (children, church, kitchen). A major decline in the German birth rate in the 1920s led to fears that racial 'inferiors' might 'out-birth' the German 'master race'. Therefore a raft of measures were introduced to encourage German women to have more children. Abortion was prohibited and restrictions placed on the acquisition of contraceptives. Financial incentives were given to families which had large numbers of children. Mothers who had large families were held in esteem and given an award: the Mothers' Cross. ~~Those who had four children got a bronze medal, those with five a silver medal and those with six or more a gold medal.~~ Nazi birth-encouraging policies were successful. In 1936 there were 30 per cent more births than there had been in 1933. Ironically, given the regime's goals, the number of employed women actually increased after 1937. This was because the Nazi regime was doing well economically. ~~Its efforts to produce 'guns' (for war) and 'butter' (an improved standard of living) meant there was a labour shortage.~~ This drew many females into work. Hitler worried about this. He continued to believe that a woman's place was in the home. Given his views, little was done for equal rights for women between 1933 and 1939.

Theme 2 Economic change in Germany and West Germany, 1871–1990

Page 93, Develop the detail

After 1923 the German economy revived. Germany introduced a new currency – **the *Rentenmark*. The currency, based on Germany's agricultural property and industrial resources, was supervised by a specially constituted authority, the *Rentenbank*, which issued a loan to the *Reichsbank*. As a result of the government's careful housekeeping and responsible fiscal policy, the new currency quickly stabilised and the *Rentenmark* was converted back into *Reichsmarks* in August 1924. The stabilisation of the currency meant that economic life quickly revived.** New reparation plans – **the Dawes Plan (1924) and the Young Plan (1929)** – enabled Germany to pay reparations. Foreigners, **particularly Americans**, invested money in Germany. By 1928 industrial production levels exceeded those of 1913. But there were some problems. German agriculture, for example, did badly, **largely as a collapse of world food prices. Moreover, Germany's reliance on international loans was potentially dangerous. Germany's economic well-being was increasingly dependent on, and vulnerable to, the investment whims of foreign capital.**

Page 99, Complete the paragraph

Between 1945 and 1949 Germany was divided into four zones and governed by the USA, Britain, France and the Soviet Union. The USA, in particular, soon aimed to restore the German economy, hoping that West Germany would then be a major ally against Communist expansion. In 1947 the US Secretary of State George Marshall offered economic aid to Europe. West Germany ultimately received nearly $1.5 billion in aid. The USA (and Britain) also helped Germany establish a new currency – the *Deutschmark*. **In this way, the intervention of the Western Allies helped to put the West German economy back on its feet, paving the way for the German economic miracle of the 1950s.**

Mark schemes

For some of the activities in the book it will be useful to refer to the mark scheme. Paper 3 requires two mark schemes, one for the AO1 assessments in Section B and C and another for Section A's AO2 assessment.

AO1 mark scheme

REVISED

- **Analytical focus**
- **Accurate detail**
- **Supported judgement**
- Argument and structure

AS		A Level
1–4	**Level 1** • **Simplistic, limited focus** • **Limited detail, limited accuracy** • **No judgement or asserted judgement** • Limited organisation, no argument	1–3
5–10	**Level 2** • **Descriptive, implicit focus** • **Limited detail, mostly accurate** • **Judgement with limited support** • Basic organisation, limited argument	4–7
11–16	**Level 3** • **Some analysis, clear focus (maybe descriptive in places)** • **Some detail, mostly accurate** • **Judgement with some support, based on implicit criteria** • Some organisation, the argument is broadly clear	11–16
17–20	**Level 4** • **Clear analysis, clear focus (maybe uneven)** • **Sufficient detail, mostly accurate** • **Judgement with some support, based on valid criteria** • Generally well organised, logical argument (may lack precision)	13–16
	Level 5 • **Sustained analysis, clear focus** • **Sufficient accurate detail, fully answers the question** • **Judgement with full support, based on valid criteria (considers relative significance)** • Well organised, logical argument communicated with precision.	17–20

A02 mark scheme

- **Analytical focus**
- **Accurate detail**
- **Supported judgement**

Level	Marks	Description
1	1–3	• Surface level comprehension of the source, demonstrated by quoting or paraphrasing, without analysis. • Some relevant knowledge of the historical context is included, but links to the source are limited. • Either no overall evaluation of the source, or discussion of reliability and utility is very basic.
2	4–7	• Some understanding of the source, demonstrated by selecting and summarising relevant information. • Some relevant knowledge of the historical context is added to the source to support or challenge the detail it includes. • An overall judgement is presented, but with limited support. Discussion of reliability and utility are based on a limited discussion of provenance and may reflect invalid assumptions.
3	8–12	• Understanding of the source, demonstrated by some analysis of key points, explaining their meaning and valid inferences. • Relevant knowledge of the historical context is used to support inferences. Contextual knowledge is also used to expand on, support, or challenge matters of detail from the source. • An overall judgement is presented, which relates to the nature and purpose of the source. The judgement is based on valid criteria, but the support is likely to be limited.
4	13–16	• Analysis of the source, demonstrated by examining the evidence to make reasoned inferences. Valid distinctions are made between information and opinion. Treatment of the two enquiries may be uneven. • Relevant knowledge of the historical context is used to reveal and discuss the limitations of the source's content. The answer attempts to interpret the source material in the context of the values and assumptions of the society it comes from. • Evaluation of the source reflects how much weight the evidence of the source can bear. Evaluation is based on valid criteria. Aspects of the judgement may have limited support.
5	17–20	• Confident interrogation of the source, in relation to both enquiries, demonstrated by reasoned inferences. The answer shows a range of ways the source can be used, making valid distinctions between information and opinion. • Relevant knowledge of the historical context is used to reveal and discuss the limitations of the source's content. The answer interprets the source material in the context of the values and assumptions of the society it comes from. • Evaluation of the source reflects how much weight the evidence of the source can bear and may distinguish between the degrees to which aspects of the source can be useful. Evaluation is based on valid criteria.